W9-CNR-346

Michael Miller

Sams **Teach Yourself**

Spotify®

in **10 Minutes**

SAMS | 800 East 96th Street, Indianapolis, Indiana 46240

Sams Teach Yourself Spotify® in 10 Minutes

Copyright © 2012 by Pearson Education, Inc.

ISBN-13: 978-0-672-33599-0
ISBN-10: 0-672-33599-9

Library of Congress Cataloging-in-Publication Data

Miller, Michael, 1958-

Sams teach yourself Spotify in 10 minutes / Michael Miller.

p. cm.

Includes index.

ISBN 978-0-672-33599-0

1. Spotify. 2. Digital jukebox software. I. Title. II. Title: Teach yourself Spotify in 10 minutes. III. Title: Spotify in 10 minutes.

ML74.4.S64M55 2012

006.5—dc23

2012005704

Printed in the United States of America

First Printing: March 2012

Trademarks

All terms mentioned in this book that are known to be trademarks or service marks have been appropriately capitalized. Sams Publishing cannot attest to the accuracy of this information. Use of a term in this book should not be regarded as affecting the validity of any trademark or service mark.

Warning and Disclaimer

Every effort has been made to make this book as complete and as accurate as possible, but no warranty or fitness is implied. The information provided is on an "as is" basis. The author and the publisher shall have neither liability nor responsibility to any person or entity with respect to any loss or damages arising from the information contained in this book.

Bulk Sales

Sams Publishing offers excellent discounts on this book when ordered in quantity for bulk purchases or special sales. For more information, please contact

U.S. Corporate and Government Sales

1-800-382-3419

corpsales@pearsontechgroup.com

For sales outside of the U.S., please contact

International Sales

international@pearsoned.com

Editor-in-Chief
Greg Wiegand

Acquisitions Editor
Michelle Newcomb

Development Editor
Robin Drake

Managing Editor
Sandra Schroeder

Project Editor
Mandie Frank

Copy Editor
Charlotte Kughen

Indexer
Erika Millen

Proofreader
Leslie Joseph

Technical Editor
Vince Averello

Publishing Coordinator
Cindy Teeters

Designer
Gary Adair

Compositor
Mark Shirar

Contents

About the Author

Michael Miller has written more than 100 nonfiction books over the past two decades. His best-selling titles include *Facebook for Grown-Ups*, *Sams Teach Yourself YouTube in 10 Minutes*, *Sams Teach Yourself Wikipedia in 10 Minutes*, *Sams Teach Yourself Google Analytics in 10 Minutes*, *Absolute Beginner's Guide to Computer Basics*, and *The Ultimate Guide to Digital Music*.

Mr. Miller has established a reputation for practical advice, technical accuracy, and an unerring empathy for the needs of his readers. For more information about Mr. Miller and his writing, visit his website at www.molehillgroup.com or email him at spotify@molehillgroup.com.

Dedication

To Sherry: Another ten minutes for us.

Acknowledgments

Special thanks to the usual suspects at Sams, including but not limited to Michelle Newcomb, Greg Wiegand, Robin Drake, Mandie Frank, and Charlotte Kughen. Thanks as well to technical editor Vince Averello, who helped ensure the technical accuracy of this book, and to my various Spotify friends for sharing their music with me.

We Want to Hear from You!

As the reader of this book, *you* are our most important critic and commentator. We value your opinion and want to know what we're doing right, what we could do better, what areas you'd like to see us publish in, and any other words of wisdom you're willing to pass our way.

As an editor-in-chief for Sams Publishing, I welcome your comments. You can email or write me directly to let me know what you did or didn't like about this book—as well as what we can do to make our books better.

Please note that I cannot help you with technical problems related to the topic of this book. We do have a User Services group, however, where I will forward specific technical questions related to the book.

When you write, please be sure to include this book's title and author as well as your name, email address, and phone number. I will carefully review your comments and share them with the author and editors who worked on the book.

Email: feedback@samspublishing.com

Mail: Greg Wiegand
         Editor-in-Chief
         Sams Publishing
         800 East 96th Street
         Indianapolis, IN 46240 USA

Reader Services

Visit our website and register this book at
www.informit.com/title/9780672335990 for convenient access to any
updates, downloads, or errata that might be available for this book.

Introduction

If you're like me, you're a music lover. I love all types and styles of music, from classic soul to intelligent pop to straight ahead jazz to... well, you name it, I probably have some of it in my collection.

Yes, I have a big music collection, but I'm always on the lookout for new music to listen to. In the past year I've been turned on to Mumford & Sons, Nikki Jean, Janelle Monae, and Mayer Hawthorne—and enjoyed new albums from some of my old favorites, such as Fountains of Wayne, Jimmy Webb, and Brian Wilson.

Where do I discover new music these day? Unfortunately, the age of the hip local record store and its savvy staff are long gone, so I have to find other ways to learn about the latest bands and trends.

Which leads me to the subject of this book. Spotify is a cool streaming music service that makes it easy to listen to all the music you like, anywhere you have an Internet connection. I listen to Spotify at home on my desktop computer, while I'm working on my laptop, and while I'm on the go with my iPhone.

But Spotify is more than that. Spotify is a great way to find out about new music I haven't heard before. Not only do I get exposed to new music and artists, I can also check them out without having to purchase a single track, let alone an entire album.

This is one of the joys of a streaming music service like Spotify, of course. You get all the music you can listen to for one low monthly fee. In fact, if you don't mind living with a few limitations, you can listen to Spotify for free. That's not a bad deal at all.

If you're a music lover, then, you owe it to yourself to check out Spotify and all you can do. Which leads us to the book you hold in your hands— *Sams Teach Yourself Spotify in 10 Minutes*. I like to think of it as the guide to Spotify you'd get if Spotify actually offered an instruction manual. (Which they don't.)

What You Need to Know Before You Use This Book

How much prior experience do you need before starting this book? Not much at all. I assume that you're familiar with the basics of listening to music online, and that you have a computer of some sort and know how to work it. Beyond that, I don't assume you're at all familiar with Spotify— the purpose of this book, after all, is to teach you about what Spotify does, and how. I take you from a basic overview of the Spotify service and its three different subscription plans all the way through advanced use of the service in a step-by-step fashion, teaching you everything you need to know along the way.

About the *Sams Teach Yourself in 10 Minutes* Series

Sams Teach Yourself Spotify in 10 Minutes uses a series of short lessons that walk you through the various features of Spotify. Each lesson is designed to take about 10 minutes, and each is limited to a particular operation or group of features. Most of the instruction is presented in easy-to-follow numbered steps, and there are plenty of examples and screen shots to show you what things look like along the way. By the time you finish this book, you should feel confident in using Spotify to listen to your favorite tunes—and to discover new music you might like.

Special Sidebars

In addition to the normal text and figures, you find what we call *sidebars* scattered throughout the lessons that highlight special kinds of information. These are intended to help you save time and to teach you important information fast.

NOTE: Notes present pertinent pieces of information related to the surrounding discussion.

TIP: Tips present advice you might find useful during execution of the current process.

CAUTION: Cautions present warnings you should heed before proceeding.

LESSON 1

Introducing Spotify

In this lesson, you learn all about the Spotify streaming music service.

What Is Spotify—and What Does It Do?

Spotify is the latest online music service to hit the U.S. It lets you stream music to any computer or mobile device, so you can listen to all the music you like from any place you happen to be. (Figure 1.1 shows the Spotify home page.)

FIGURE 1.1   Welcome to Spotify.

NOTE: **Spotify in Europe**

Although Spotify is new to the U.S., it's an established service in Europe; it was launched in Sweden in October of 2008, and today has more than 10 million European users. That makes Spotify one of the world's largest online music services, right up there with iTunes and Pandora. It launched in the U.S. in July of 2011.

Unlike iTunes, which is essentially an online music store for digital downloads, Spotify is a streaming music service. That means you have immediate access to all the music stored in Spotify's online database, for one low monthly fee. You don't pay for each download; instead, your subscription covers all the music you listen to in a given month.

Currently, Spotify offers more than 15 million individual tracks for streaming, from all four major music labels and a large number of independent labels. You can find everything from the latest pop and hip hop hits to classic rock tunes, country and bluegrass, and even jazz and classical music.

In addition, Spotify consolidates its online music database with music you've previously downloaded or ripped to your PC. When you first install the Spotify software, it scans your hard disk for existing tracks and creates a Local Files library. You can then create playlists that combine tunes on your PC with tunes you stream from Spotify. (Figure 1.2 shows a local library in Spotify.)

In this regard, Spotify plays well with your iPod or iPhone and any tracks you've purchased from the iTunes Store. (The Spotify application even looks a little like iTunes.) Spotify plays less well with Windows Media Player, as it's not compatible with Windows's .wma audio file format.

NOTE: **A Word About (In)compatibility**

Spotify is compatible with music stored in Apple's .m4a file format, as well as the universal .mp3 format. It is not compatible with Windows's .wma file format.

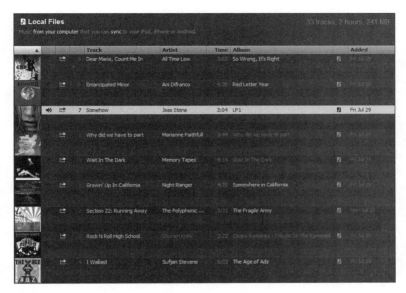

FIGURE 1.2   Listening to local files with Spotify.

Listening to a tune is as easy as searching or browsing for it from within Spotify and then double-clicking the song's title. Playback is through your device's built-in speakers.

How Is Spotify Different from iTunes?

Given the popularity of iPods, iPhones, and iPads, chances are you're familiar with Apple's iTunes music player. iTunes is an application that lets you play and manage all your digital music, with special emphasis on purchasing and downloading music from Apple's iTunes Store.

Even though the interfaces are similar, Spotify is much different from iTunes in that it's a subscription service, not a download service. It's a totally different model for listening to music.

With iTunes, you purchase and download the individual tracks you want. You pay anywhere from $0.69 to $1.29 per track, and the music files are then downloaded to and stored on your computer. After you purchase a track, you own and can play it back on a specified number of other devices.

Spotify, however, is a streaming music subscription service. You don't pay by the track; instead, you pay a set monthly fee. This enables you to listen to as much music as you want anytime you want (within the limits of the plan you subscribe to, of course).

The upside of Spotify versus iTunes is definitely cost. Spotify's basic plan is free, and even its most expensive plan costs only $9.99 per month. You'll pay that much (or more) if you purchase just 10 tracks from the iTunes Store. Spotify is an "all you can eat" service, which is very attractive to frequent listeners.

The only downside of Spotify's streaming approach is that you don't actually own the music you listen to. It's more like listening to a radio station than listening to your own CDs—albeit a very personalized station, and one where you control the programming. If Spotify wants or has to pull a song from its service, that song is no longer available to you.

As to selection, Spotify and iTunes are neck and neck. iTunes has around 20 million songs available for download, whereas Spotify has 15 million tunes in its collection. It's likely you'll find a similar selection with both services.

So if you're a heavy music listener, Spotify is a definite alternative to iTunes. Plus, it's fully compatible with your iPod, iPhone, or iPad.

How Is Spotify Different from Pandora?

It's obvious that Spotify represents a different way to listen to music than does iTunes. In this regard, Spotify is more like other streaming music services, such as Pandora.

If you're a music lover, you might have heard about Pandora (www.pandora.com). Like Spotify, Pandora streams music in real time to any computer connected to the Internet. Unlike Spotify, Pandora offers in-app purchasing if you hear a track you really like and want to own.

Instead of playlists, Pandora lets you create personalized "stations." You select one or more tracks or artists, and Pandora creates a new station programmed for your specific tastes. For example, if you're a big fan of Katy Perry, Pandora creates a station called Katy Perry Radio, filled with tracks from Ms. Perry and similar artists. (Spotify offers similar functionality with its Spotify Radio feature, but with the ability to skip an unlimited number of tracks; Pandora only lets you skip six tracks each hour, or twelve in a day.)

In terms of selection, Pandora only has 900,000 tracks in its database, compared to Spotify's 15 million; that's a huge difference. The result is that you're likely to notice a lot of tracks and artists are missing from Pandora's service, compared to what you'll find with Spotify.

As to cost, Pandora is free—up to 80 hours per week, which is probably more than you'd listen, anyway. Past that point, you pay $.99 for unlimited streaming. That contrasts with Spotify's Free plan (20 hours per month at no charge) or $4.99 Unlimited streaming plan.

Although Spotify ends up being more expensive than Pandora for most users, you get a lot more selection. If you find yourself being frustrated by what's missing from Pandora, give Spotify a spin—there's a lot more there to listen to.

Social Sharing with Spotify

Another big difference between Spotify and other music services is that it's much more social. Spotify integrates tightly with Facebook—in fact, you sign into Spotify with your Facebook ID and password. You can then share the songs and playlists you listen to with your Facebook friends, as shown in Figure 1.3. After you link your Spotify and Facebook accounts, all this sharing takes place automatically.

FIGURE 1.3   Sharing your Spotify music.

You can also share the music you listen to with your friends via Twitter or via email; they can share their tracks with you, too. That makes Spotify a very social music network—and a great way to find out what your friends are listening to.

Extending Spotify with Third-Party Apps

Spotify is more than just a database of songs, however. It also offers an "open" platform that other companies can use to offer additional services to listeners, in the form of free apps that can be added to the Spotify interface.

For example, *Rolling Stone* magazine offers an app that recommends music you might like, as shown in Figure 1.4; Songkick offers an app that tracks and notifies you of local performances from your favorite artists. These third-party apps add a lot of functionality to Spotify and help you expand your listening.

How Much Does Spotify Cost?

Using Spotify is as easy as signing up for one of their subscription plans, installing the Spotify software (it runs on both Windows and Mac PCs), and then connecting to Spotify and selecting what music you want to listen to. If you subscribe to Spotify's top plan, you can even stream music to

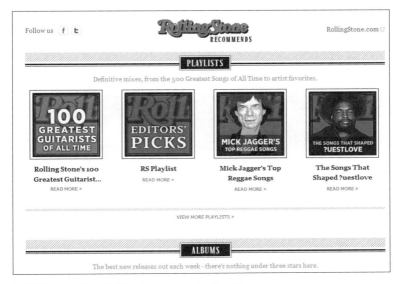

FIGURE 1.4   The Rolling Stone app for Spotify.

your iPhone or Android phone, thanks to native apps on both smartphone platforms.

As you learn in the next lesson, Spotify offers three different subscription plans. These range in cost from free to $9.99 per month, depending on the level of service you require. It's a low-cost way to listen to all the music you love—on either your computer or mobile device.

Summary

In this lesson, you learned what Spotify is and what it does. In the next lesson you learn about Spotify's three subscription plans.

LESSON 2

Choosing a Subscription Plan

In this lesson, you learn about Spotify's three subscription plans.

Understanding Spotify's Subscription Plans

To use the Spotify music service, you have to sign up as a subscriber, and then download the Spotify software. Spotify offers three levels of subscription access, ranging in price from free to $9.99 per month. The more you pay, the more music you get to listen to.

The three plans are as follows:

▶ **Free.** This is no doubt the most popular plan because you don't have to pay anything to use it. This plan displays occasional ads in the application, as shown in Figure 2.1, and comes with some limitations—there's no mobile version, you can't use it in offline mode, and you're limited to 20 hours of listening each month.

▶ **Unlimited.** This plan costs $4.99 per month and eliminates both the ads from the interface and the listening time limit. (Figure 2.2 shows Spotify without the ads.) With this plan you can listen to your music as long and as often as you like. However, there is still no mobile component to this plan.

▶ **Premium.** This is Spotify's ultimate plan, at $9.99 per month. This plan gives you everything you get with the Unlimited plan and adds access via your mobile devices, as well as the ability to listen to your own music while offline. You also get enhanced sound quality, which makes all your music sound better, and the ability to play Spotify through whole-house media players, such as those offered by Sonos, Squeezebox, and Boxee.

FIGURE 2.1   Spotify Free, complete with in-app advertising.

FIGURE 2.2   Spotify Unlimited and Premium—no ads.

Table 2.1 compares the details of each plan.

TABLE 2.1   Spotify's Subscription Plans

Feature	Free Plan	Unlimited Plan	Premium Plan
Monthly cost	Free	$4.99	$9.99
Number of streaming tracks available	15 million	15 million	15 million
Play local music files from your PC	Yes	Yes	Yes
Number of listening hours per month	20 hours	Unlimited	Unlimited
Spotify radio	Yes	Yes	Yes
Advertising supported	Yes	No	No
Spotify social sharing	Yes	Yes	Yes
Offline listening mode	No	No	Yes
Enhanced audio quality	No	No	Yes
Exclusive content	No	No	Yes
Play your music in other countries	14 days only	Yes	Yes
Listening on mobile devices	No	No	Yes
Play local files on your mobile device	No	No	Yes
Play Spotify on Sonos, Squeezebox, and other media players	No	No	Yes

Which Plan Is Best for You?

Which of these plans you should choose depends on how much music you like to listen to, and where.

If you're only an occasional listener (20 hours or less per month), go with the Free plan. This plan is also good if you just want to check out the Spotify service before you make a more significant commitment—and if you don't mind seeing ads while you browse for tunes. Not surprisingly, the majority of Spotify members use the Free service.

If you're a heavier listener (more than 20 hours a month), go with the $4.99/month Unlimited plan. This is also the plan to use if you get annoyed by onscreen advertising; it's an ad-free plan.

If you want to listen to Spotify on your iPhone, smartphone, or other mobile device, you need to go with the $9.99/month Premium plan. This is the only plan that offers streaming to mobile devices; it also lets you create and listen to playlists when you're not connected to the Internet.

NOTE: **Changing Plans**

You have to choose a plan when you first sign up for Spotify. However, you can change plans at any time in the future. For more details, see Lesson 4, "Editing Your Profile and Account Information."

Summary

In this lesson, you learned about Spotify's subscription plans. In the next lesson you learn how to sign up and start using the Spotify service.

LESSON 3
Signing Up and Getting Started

In this lesson, you learn how to sign up for and start using Spotify.

Downloading and Installing Spotify

Spotify is an online service that you access via a software application you install on your computer. The first part of the sign-up process involves downloading and installing the Spotify software.

Follow these steps:

1. From your web browser, go to www.spotify.com.

2. From the main Spotify page, shown in Figure 3.1, click the Download Spotify button.

FIGURE 3.1   Getting ready to download and install the Spotify software.

> NOTE: **Different Versions Look Different**
>
> Depending on your computer and the version of Spotify you're installing, your screen might look somewhat different from the figures shown here, but the operations should be approximately the same.

3. The download should start automatically. If prompted to run or save the file, click the Run button. (Depending on your software setup, you might need to click Run a second time in another dialog box.)

4. Follow the instructions to install the Spotify software on your computer.

> NOTE: **Operating Systems**
>
> At present, the Spotify software is available for computers running the Windows XP/Vista/7 and Mac OS X 10.5.0 or higher operating systems.

Creating a Spotify Account

You log into Spotify with your Facebook account. If you do not yet use Facebook, you'll need to become a Facebook member before you can join Spotify.

You sign up for your Spotify account from Spotify's website. Follow these steps:

1. Go to www.spotify.com.

2. Click the Log In button at the top of the screen and then click the Log In with Facebook button.

> NOTE: **Alternative Method**
>
> You can also create a Spotify account by launching the Spotify software and clicking the Not a User? Sign Up link on the log-in screen.

3. When the Facebook Log In dialog box appears, as shown in Figure 3.2, enter your email address and Facebook password into the appropriate boxes and then click the Log In button.

FIGURE 3.2   Logging into Spotify with your Facebook account.

4. You now see the screen shown in Figure 3.3. Click the Log In button.

FIGURE 3.3   Linking your Spotify and Facebook accounts.

You are now registered as a Spotify user with a Free account. You can change your subscription plan later, if you like.

Launching Spotify

You access the Spotify music service via the Spotify software you just installed. To launch the software and sign into Spotify (from within Windows), follow these steps:

1. Click the Windows orb to open the Start menu.

2. Click All Programs.

3. Click Spotify.

4. When the Spotify log-in screen appears, as shown in Figure 3.4, enter your Facebook email and password and then click the blue Log In button.

FIGURE 3.4   Logging into Spotify.

NOTE: **Remember Me**

If you want Spotify to remember your username on future visits, check the Remember Me box on the log in screen.

Spotify now logs you into your account and launches the Spotify software. At this point Spotify may also display a Welcome to Spotify screen with the opportunity to take a tour and start configuring various options. Feel free to take the tour, or skip the tour and use Spotify at your own speed.

Summary

In this lesson, you learned how to download the Spotify software and create an account. In the next lesson you learn how to edit your account details.

LESSON 4

Editing Your Profile and Account Information

In this lesson, you learn how to edit your Spotify profile and change your subscription plan.

Editing Your Account Profile

Spotify creates a user profile based on the information it receives from your Facebook account. You can edit this profile at any time from any web browser.

Follow these steps:

1. From within the Spotify software, select Help > Your Account—or go directly to https://www.spotify.com/us/account/profile/ in your web browser.

2. When the Your Account page appears, as shown in Figure 4.1, click Edit Profile in the menu bar.

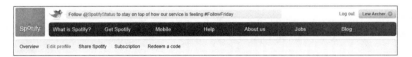

FIGURE 4.1   Viewing your account information.

3. When the Edit Your Profile page appears, scroll to the Personal Information section, shown in Figure 4.2.

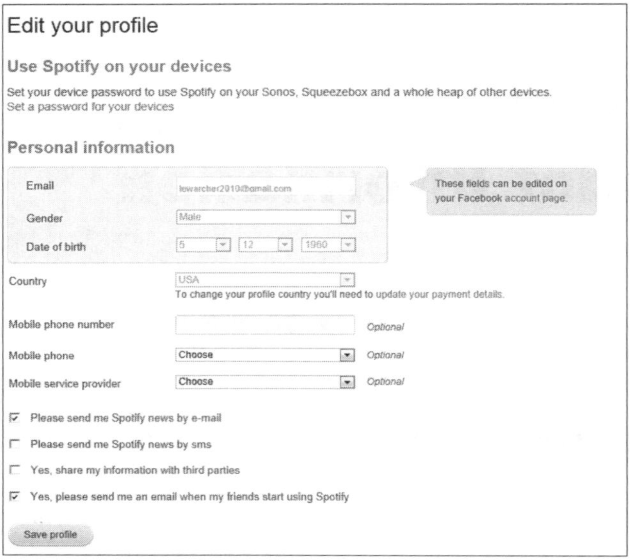

Edit your profile

Use Spotify on your devices

Set your device password to use Spotify on your Sonos, Squeezebox and a whole heap of other devices.
Set a password for your devices

Personal information

Email	lowarcher2019@gmail.com	These fields can be edited on your Facebook account page.
Gender	Male	
Date of birth	5 12 1960	

Country   USA
To change your profile country you'll need to update your payment details.

Mobile phone number   [   ]   *Optional*

Mobile phone   Choose   *Optional*

Mobile service provider   Choose   *Optional*

☑ Please send me Spotify news by e-mail

☐ Please send me Spotify news by sms

☐ Yes, share my information with third parties

☑ Yes, please send me an email when my friends start using Spotify

[Save profile]

FIGURE 4.2   Editing your profile information.

NOTE: **You Can't Change These**

The top three fields—Email, Gender, and Date of Birth—are linked directly with your Facebook account and cannot be edited from Spotify. You must edit these fields from within your Facebook account. In addition, to change your country, you first have to update your payment status.

---

4. To display your mobile phone number, enter that number into the Mobile Phone Number box.

5. To tell Spotify what kind of mobile phone you're using, pull down the Mobile Phone list and make a selection.

6. To tell Spotify what mobile service provider you're using, pull down the Mobile Service Provider list and make a selection.

7. To receive Spotify news via email (sent to the email address you use for your Facebook account), check the Please Send Me Spotify News by E-Mail box.

8. To receive Spotify news via text message on your mobile phone, check the Please Send Me Spotify News by SMS box.

9. To let Spotify share your personal information with other companies, check the Yes, Share My Information with Third Parties box.

10. To receive a notification when your Facebook friends sign up for Spotify, check the Yes, Please Send Me an Email When My Friends Start Using Spotify box.

11. Click the Save Profile button.

Changing Your Subscription Plan and Payment Information

When you first signed up for Spotify, you probably subscribed to the Free plan, which limits you to just 20 hours of use per month. To change your subscription plan, follow these steps:

> NOTE: **Subscription Plans**
>
> Spotify offers three subscription plans—Free, Unlimited, and Premium. Learn more in Lesson 2, "Choosing a Subscription Plan."

1. From within the Spotify software, select Help > Your Account— or go directly to https://www.spotify.com/us/account/profile/ in your web browser.

2. When the Your Account page appears, click Subscription in the menu bar.

3. As shown in Figure 4.3, the Your Subscription page displays your current subscription level in the Subscription Status section. To change your subscription level, click either Spotify Unlimited or Spotify Premium.

4. When the next page appears, as shown in Figure 4.4, select a payment method—either Visa/MasterCard/American Express or PayPal—then click the Continue button.

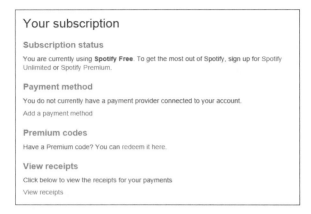

FIGURE 4.3   Viewing—and changing—your subscription information.

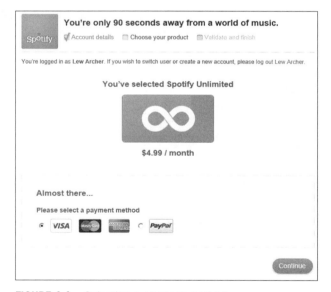

FIGURE 4.4   Selecting a payment method.

5. If you selected credit card payment, you now see the screen shown in Figure 4.5. Enter your credit card number, expiration date, and CVC number and then click the Confirm Payment button.

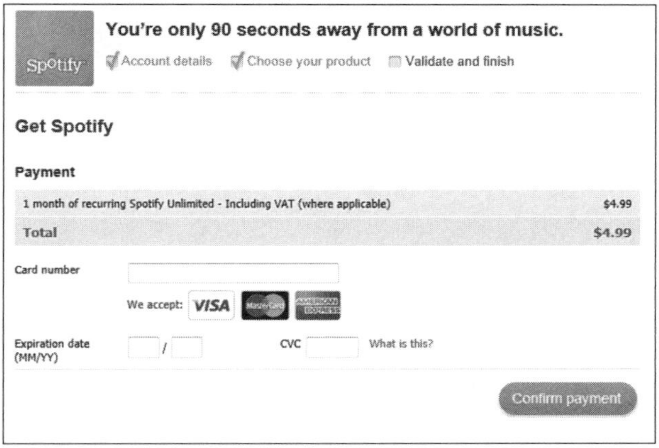

You're only 90 seconds away from a world of music.

Spotify   ☑ Account details   ☑ Choose your product   ☐ Validate and finish

Get Spotify

Payment

1 month of recurring Spotify Unlimited - Including VAT (where applicable)	$4.99
Total	$4.99

Card number

We accept: **VISA**

Expiration date   /   CVC   What is this?
(MM/YY)

Confirm payment

FIGURE 4.5   Entering your credit card information.

NOTE: **CVC**

The CVC (card verification code) is a three-digit number found printed on the back of your MasterCard or Visa card, or a four-digit number found printed on the front of your American Express card.

---

6. If you selected PayPal payment, you now see the screen shown in Figure 4.6. Enter the email address and password for your PayPal account and then click the Log In button and follow the onscreen instructions to complete your payment.

Your account is now upgraded to the subscription level you selected. Your credit card or PayPal account will be billed each month for the amount of your subscription plan.

NOTE: **Downgrading to a Free Account**

At any time you can downgrade your account to the Free level. Go to the Your Subscription page, scroll to the Manage Your Subscriptions section, and click View Your Options. From there you can easily change to another plan.

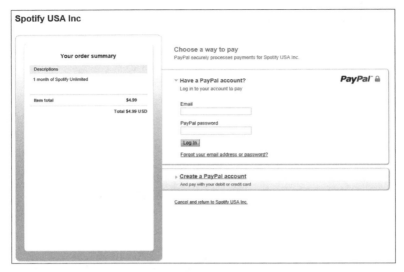

FIGURE 4.6   Entering your PayPal payment information.

Summary

In this lesson, you learned how to edit your account information and change your subscription level. In the next lesson you learn how to find your way around the Spotify application.

LESSON 5

Navigating Spotify

In this lesson, you learn to find your way around the Spotify software.

Getting Around Spotify

When you launch Spotify, the application opens and connects via the Internet to the Spotify service. You need to be connected to use Spotify; all the music you listen to is streamed live over the Internet.

The Spotify application consists of a menu and navigation bar at the top; three panes in the middle; and a set of playback controls at the bottom. We'll look at each of these sections individually.

Menu and Navigation Bar

Across the top of the Spotify software is a set of pull-down menus and, beneath that, a set of navigation controls. This section, shown in Figure 5.1, is the menu and navigation bar.

FIGURE 5.1   Spotify's menu and navigation bar.

The menu bar consists of five pull-down menus that you use to access specific functionality:

 ▶ **File.** Pull down this menu to access playlist-related features, enter a private session, log out from the Spotify service, and exit the Spotify software.

 ▶ **Edit.** Pull down this menu to access standard cut/copy/delete functionality, edit track information, mark items as seen, search for music, and edit your Spotify preferences.

▶ **View.** Pull down this menu to display or hide the people list and large album artwork, and to change the library view.

▶ **Playback.** Pull down this menu to access standard playback controls, shuffle and repeat, and volume up and down.

▶ **Help.** Pull down this menu to view and edit your account information and access Spotify's Help system.

Beneath the menu bar is a collection of controls for navigating Spotify. The left and right arrows at the far left help you move backward and forward through pages you've previously visited. You use the Search box to search for music to listen to. And you click your name or picture to view and edit your Spotify profile, enter a private session, view and edit your Spotify account, and log out of the Spotify service.

> NOTE: **Private Sessions**
>
> A private session is one that is not automatically shared with Facebook. Learn more about private sessions in Lesson 17, "Sharing Music with Your Friends."

Navigation Pane

The left pane in the middle of the Spotify application is the navigation pane. As you can see in Figure 5.2, this pane provides access to a variety

When the pointer
hovers over the album
artwork, an "enlarge
button" appears;
click it to increase
the size of the art.

FIGURE 5.2   Spotify's navigation pane.

of features and functions; click an item in this pane to display specific
content in the center content pane.

There are three primary sections of the navigation pane:

> ▶ **Main.** This section displays the following content: What's New,
>   People, Inbox, Play Queue, and Devices.

> ▶ **Apps.** This section provides access to Spotify's auxiliary applica-
>   tions, as well as apps from third-party developers.

> ▶ **Collection.** This section provides access to your personal
>   library—those tracks stored on your computer that you've synced
>   to Spotify. This section also displays any playlists you've created.

At the bottom of the navigation pane is the now playing section—the
album cover for the track you're currently listening to. You can display the
album art at its default small size (as shown in Figure 5.2), or see a much
larger version (as shown in Figure 5.3) by hovering the pointer over the art
and clicking the "enlarge button" that appears. After you enlarge the album
art, the "enlarge button" becomes a "reduce button" that you can click to
return to the miniature version.

FIGURE 5.3   The navigation pane with larger "now playing" artwork.

Main Content Pane

The content you select in the navigation pane is displayed in the center content pane. For example, if you select What's New in the navigation pane, you see Spotify's What's New page, which we'll discuss momentarily.

People Pane

The pane at the far right of the Spotify window, shown in Figure 5.4, is the people pane, or what Spotify calls the *people list*. The top half of this pane displays your favorite friends—those Spotify and Facebook friends you've opted to share music with. The bottom half of the pane displays tracks recently listened to by these friends.

FIGURE 5.4   Spotify's people pane.

To view the profile of a given friend, click that friend's name in the people pane and then click View Profile. To listen to a track that a friend has listened or is listening to, click that item in the people pane. This displays information about the track, as shown in Figure 5.5; click the play arrow in the album artwork to play the track.

FIGURE 5.5   Getting ready to listen to a track that a friend has listened to.

Playback Controls

The very bottom of the Spotify application hosts a set of playback controls, as shown in Figure 5.6. Read more about these controls in Lesson 10, "Playing Tracks and Albums."

FIGURE 5.6   Spotify's playback controls.

Viewing the Main Features

The Main section of the navigation pane provides access to five key features, which we'll discuss next.

What's New

The What's New page, shown in Figure 5.7, is Spotify's default "home" page. There's a lot of interesting content here; this is a great page to discover new music.

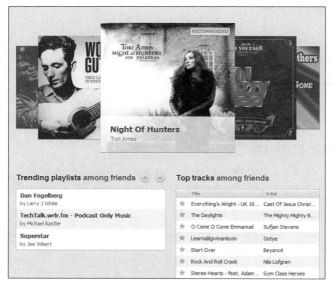

FIGURE 5.7   The cover flow view of Spotify's What's New page.

At the top of the What's New page is a selection of featured albums, in a "cover flow"-like display. Click an album on the left or right to scroll in that direction. To view all the tracks in the "front" album, hover over it and then click the album title. To play the front album, hover over it and click the playback button.

Beneath the cover flow selection are two lists. The list on the left displays Trending Playlists Among Friends—those playlists your friends are most listening to. The list on the right displays Top Tracks Among Friends, the individual tunes that your friends are listening to.

Beneath these lists is the New Releases section, shown in Figure 5.8, which displays the latest album releases, ten at a time; click the left and right arrows at the top right of this section to display more albums. To view the tracks for a given album, click that album's artwork; to play an album, hover over it and then click the playback button.

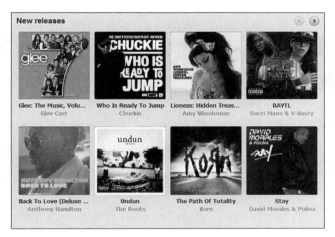

FIGURE 5.8   The New Releases section of the What's New page.

Finally, at the bottom of the What's New page, are two more lists. The left-hand list displays Playlists Near You—that is, playlists currently being played by Spotify users near your geographic location. The right-hand list displays Top Tracks Near You.

People

The People page, shown in Figure 5.9, displays one of two groups of friends. Select Everyone at the top of this page and you see all your Facebook friends' profile pictures, whether or not they belong to Spotify. Select On Spotify at the top of the page and you see only those Facebook friends who are also Spotify members.

FIGURE 5.9   Spotify's People page.

Inbox

The Inbox page, shown in Figure 5.10, displays a list of music that your
Spotify friends have sent you. For each track you see the title (song name),

FIGURE 5.10   Spotify's Inbox page.

who sent it to you (from), recording artist, length of the track (time),
album, and when it was sent to you (added). Double-click any individual
track to play that tune.

If people send you a lot of music, you can filter the tracks you see. Click the Filter button at the top of this pane and select Only Show Items from People I Follow.

> NOTE: **Unplayed Tracks**
>
> If new tracks are sent to you, they'll be highlighted with a number in red next to the Inbox item in the Main section of the navigation bar. The number indicates how many sent tracks are as of yet unplayed.

Play Queue

The Play Queue page, shown in Figure 5.11, displays those tracks you've selected but have not yet played. For each track you see the song name

FIGURE 5.11   Spotify's Play Queue page.

(track), recording artist, time, popularity (among Spotify users), and album. To jump to a track and begin playback, just double-click the track name.

Devices

You use the Devices page to sync Spotify with your iPod, iPhone, or Android device. Learn more in Lesson 22, "Synching Spotify to Your iPod."

Viewing Your Apps

The Apps section of Spotify's navigation pane provides access to a variety of add-on applications from Spotify and third-party developers. These apps provide added functionality that make it easier to find interesting music on the Spotify service.

Learn more about Spotify apps in Lesson 20, "Exploring Spotify Apps."

AppFinder

To find new apps, open the AppFinder page, shown in Figure 5.12. This page displays all currently available Spotify apps; click the Add button for an app you want to add to your version of Spotify.

FIGURE 5.12 Spotify's AppFinder page.

Top Lists

The Top Lists app, shown in Figure 5.13, is a built-in app that lists the most-played tracks and albums on the Spotify service. Double-click any track to play that track; double-click any album to view that album's tracks.

FIGURE 5.13   Spotify's Top Lists page.

Radio

Spotify's Radio app, shown in Figure 5.14, lets you create on-the-fly "radio stations" based on artists you select. You can also visit this page to view other popular Spotify radio stations, as well as listen to stations created by genre (alternative, country, hip hop, and so forth).

Learn more about Spotify radio in Lesson 12, "Playing Spotify Radio."

Individual Apps

Any apps you've added to Spotify are displayed at the bottom of the Apps section of the navigation pane. Click an app to display that app in the content pane.

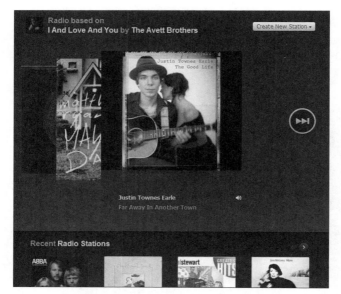

FIGURE 5.14   Spotify's Radio page.

Viewing Your Collection

Your personal music collection is accessed from the Collection section of the navigation pane. This includes playlists you've created and your own personal tracks you've added to Spotify.

Library

Your library is all your music on Spotify. The Library page, shown in Figure 5.15, displays music you've starred (marked as a favorite with a star), imported, or purchased. By default, the library is organized by artist, and then by album, although you can change the sort order by clicking the top of any given column. There are columns for track, artist, time, and album. To play a given track, double-click it.

FIGURE 5.15 Spotify's Library page.

Local Files

As you learn in Lesson 7, "Importing Your Local Music Files into Spotify," you can add music already on your computer to your Spotify account. All tracks you've imported are displayed on the Local Files page, shown in Figure 5.16. For each imported song you see the track name, artist, time, album, and when the track was imported. Double-click any track to play it.

Starred

When you find a track you particularly like, you can "star" that track—essentially labeling it as one of your favorites. All the tracks you've starred are displayed on the Starred page, shown in Figure 5.17.

FIGURE 5.16   Spotify's Local Files page.

FIGURE 5.17   Spotify's Starred page.

Playlists

At the bottom of the Collection section of the navigation pane are all the playlists you've created. These include playlists you've imported from iTunes or Windows Media Player when you imported individual tracks into Spotify. You can also create new playlists from here, by clicking the New Playlist item. Figure 5.18 shows a typical playlist; learn more about

FIGURE 5.18 A typical playlist page.

playlists in Lesson 14, "Creating and Playing Playlists."

Summary

In this lesson, you learned how to navigate within the various areas of the Spotify application. In the next lesson you learn how to personalize your version of Spotify to suit your taste and the way you like to listen to music.

LESSON 6

Personalizing Spotify

In this lesson, you learn how to personalize the look and feel of the Spotify interface. (For details on how to change the way Spotify operates, such as whether the app opens automatically at startup, see Lesson 24, "Configuring Spotify.")

Displaying or Hiding the People List

To be honest, there's not a lot about its software that Spotify lets you customize. Still, there are a few ways you can personalize Spotify for maximum enjoyment of the app's look and feel.

The first option is to hide the right-hand people pane. By default, Spotify displays this pane, as shown in Figure 6.1. But if your desktop space is at a premium, or if you don't do a lot of music sharing with friends, you may choose to hide the pane, instead.

To hide the people pane, click the View menu and uncheck the People List item. To display a hidden people pane, click View > People List.

Enlarging or Reducing the 'Now Playing' Artwork

Spotify displays the album artwork for the currently playing track at the very bottom of the navigation pane. You can display this artwork either small (shown in Figure 6.2), which takes up little space, or large (shown in Figure 6.3), which takes up more space.

To display the artwork in the large format, click the View menu and check the Large Now Playing Artwork item. To minimize the artwork, click the View menu and uncheck this item.

FIGURE 6.1   Displaying the people pane.

FIGURE 6.2   Small now playing artwork.

Displaying Your Music as an Album List

When displaying music in your collection—your library or playlists or whatever—you have the option of displaying items in a basic list, as shown in Figure 6.4, or organized by album, as shown in Figure 6.5. Some people like the album list view, as it visually groups tracks together; others prefer the efficiency of the standard list view.

FIGURE 6.3   Large now playing artwork.

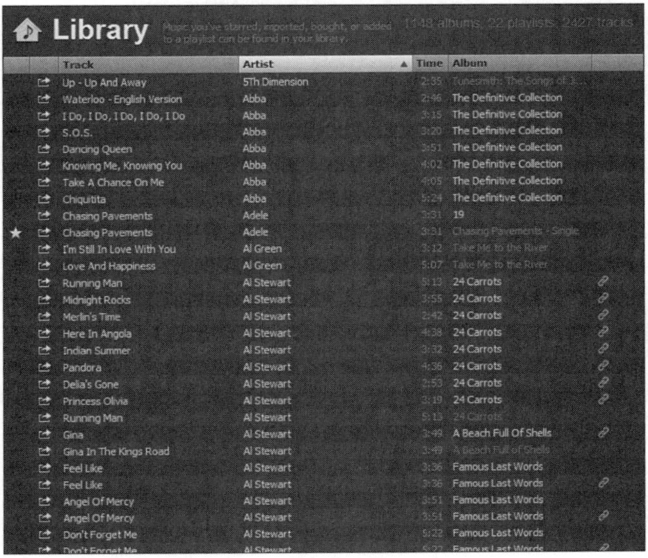

FIGURE 6.4   Tracks displayed as a basic list.

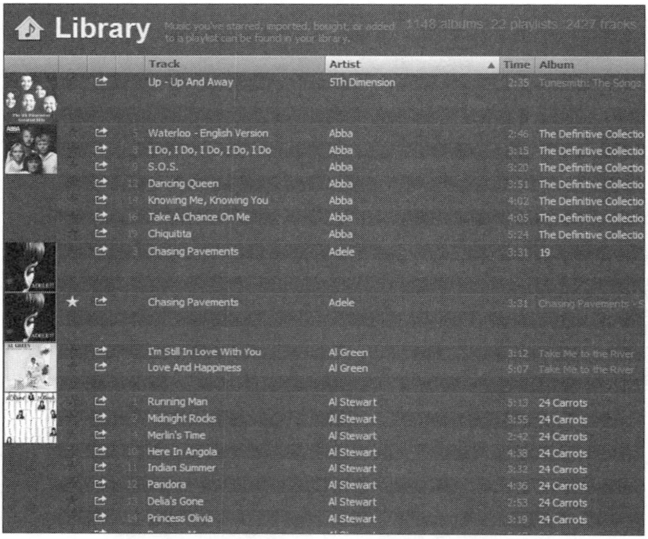

FIGURE 6.5   Tracks displayed as an album list

To display tracks as an album list, click the View menu and check the View as Album List item. To display tracks in basic list view, click the View menu and uncheck this item. Alternatively, you can press Ctrl+G on your computer keyboard to toggle between basic list view and album list view.

Displaying or Hiding Playlists in Your Profile

When another Spotify user clicks your name anywhere on the site, he or she sees your public profile. By default, your profile displays the top artists you listen to as well as any playlists you've created. You can, however, opt to hide specific playlists from public view.

To hide playlists in your profile, follow these steps:

1. Click your name or picture at the top-right corner of the Spotify window.

2. Select Profile from the pull-down menu.

3. When your profile is displayed, as shown in Figure 6.6, click the Edit button at the top right.

FIGURE 6.6   Getting ready to edit your public profile.

4. Scroll down to the playlists section of the page, as shown in Figure 6.7.

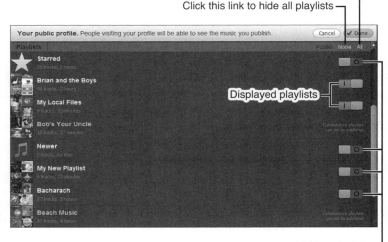

FIGURE 6.7   Showing or hiding individual playlists.

5. To display a playlist, click the right side of the hide/show button, to display the green "show" icon.

6. To hide a playlist, click the left side of the hide/show button, to display the round "hide" icon.

7. To hide all playlists, click None at the top of the Playlists list; to show all playlists, click All.

> NOTE: **Collaborative Playlists**
> Collaborative playlists are not displayed on your profile.

Summary

In this lesson, you learned how to personalize your version of Spotify. In the next lesson you learn how to import your own music into your Spotify library.

LESSON 7

Importing Your Local Music Files into Spotify

In this lesson, you learn how to import your own music into Spotify to listen to favorite music you already own, create custom playlists with your own tracks, and share those local files with your online friends.

Why Should You Import Your Music into Spotify?

One of the unique aspects of Spotify is that it blends a typical streaming music service with the playback of music you have stored on your own PC. This way you can supplement Spotify's 15 million-track library with other tracks you own that aren't available from Spotify.

Spotify lets you import tracks you've either downloaded to your PC from other websites or ripped from CDs you've purchased. In fact, when you first install the Spotify software, it can automatically scan your hard disk for existing tracks and create a Local Files library. (Spotify offers this functionality at installation, but you might prefer to import your files at a more convenient time.) After Spotify imports your local tracks, you can create playlists that combine tunes on your PC with tunes you stream from Spotify.

You can import music files in the universal .mp3 format, as well as Apple's .m4a format—which means you can consolidate your entire iTunes library into Spotify. Unfortunately, Spotify is not compatible with Windows' .wma audio file format, nor can it import files in FLAC and other lossless formats.

> TIP: **Converting Files**
>
> You can, if you like, convert your .wma or FLAC files to the .mp3 format, which can be imported into Spotify. Use a program such as Factory Audio Converter (www.myformatfactory.com) or ConverterLite (www.converterlite.com) to convert the files.

Importing Your Music Library

As noted, Spotify can automatically import all music files found in your computer's Music, iTunes, and Downloads folders. You can also configure Spotify to manually import tunes stored anywhere on your PC. Follow these steps:

1. Select Edit > Preferences.

2. When the Preferences page appears, scroll down to the Local Files section, shown in Figure 7.1.

FIGURE 7.1 Configuring Spotify to import music from local folders.

3. Checkmark the location(s) containing music you want to import.

4. To add another location, click the Add Source button. When the Browse for Folder dialog box appears, select the desired folder and click the OK button.

> TIP: **Selecting Folders**
>
> If you add a source location for local music files, Spotify imports from that specified folder and its subfolders (if any). So if you have music tucked away into all sorts of locations on your hard drive, rather than just in the My Music folder, you can consolidate all

those files with Spotify; just import the folder one level up from all the rest (typically My Documents).

When you select a new location, Spotify automatically scans that location for compatible files and imports them into the library.

NOTE: **Files Are Linked, Not Uploaded**

When Spotify "imports" a file into its library, it doesn't actually upload that file onto Spotify's servers. Instead, it links its library to that file on your computer's hard drive. For this reason, you can play local files only on the computer on which they reside, not on other computers connected to the Spotify service.

Removing Imported Files

You might find that you'd rather not mix your local music files with Spotify's streaming music. In that case, you can remove links to your local files from Spotify.

To remove individual files, follow these steps:

1. Select Local Files in the Collection section of Spotify's navigation pane.

2. Right-click the file you want to remove and select Delete from the pop-up menu. Alternatively, select the file and press Delete on your computer keyboard.

When you delete a file, it is no longer displayed in the Local Files list, and isn't playable if you include it in a playlist. The file itself, however, is not physically deleted from your computer—which means you can reimport it at a later time if you want.

You can also remove all files from a particular location on your hard drive. Follow these steps:

1. Select Edit, Preferences.

2. When the Preferences page appears, scroll to the Local Files section.

3. Uncheck those locations that you want to remove from Spotify.

Viewing and Playing Your Imported Music

All of the files you import from your computer are stored in Spotify's Local Files library. To view the files you've imported, select Local Files in the Collection section of Spotify's navigation pane. All imported files are flagged by an icon of a musical note, as shown in Figure 7.2.

FIGURE 7.2   Viewing imported tracks in your Local Files library.

To play a local file, you have to be logged onto Spotify from the computer that hosts that file. There are two ways to begin playback. You can double-click the file, or you can right-click the file and select Play from the pop-up menu. (In addition, after you've started playing one track, you can play another track by selecting the file and then clicking the Play button in the transport controls.)

> NOTE: **Commercials**
>
> Spotify typically inserts commercials after every few tracks of streaming music. The service will *not*, however, insert commercials when you're listening to your own local files.

Listening to Local Files on Your Mobile Device

You can also use your compatible mobile device to listen to local files stored on your computer—if both your PC and mobile device are connected to the same Wi-Fi network.

To listen to local files on your mobile device, follow these steps:

1. On your computer, create a playlist that contains the local music you want to listen to on your mobile device.

2. Connect your mobile device to the same Wi-Fi network that your computer is connected to.

3. Launch the Spotify app on your mobile device and mark the newly created playlist as an Offline Playlist.

The playlist you selected is now available for playback on your mobile device.

Sharing Local Files

Spotify is big on sharing music with your friends. But how can you share your own local music with your Spotify or Facebook friends?

Although you can't share any tunes that Spotify doesn't offer on its own service, you can share the *titles* of tracks you have stored locally. Here's how it works:

▶ If Spotify has in its database a track you have also imported into your Spotify account, you can share that track with friends.

▶ If a track you've imported is *not* also in Spotify's database, the title of the track is shared with your friends, either on a standalone basis or as part of a shared playlist.

▶ If a track you've imported is not in Spotify's database but *is* already stored on your friend's computer (and imported into his or her Spotify account), then that track is playable when you share it.

NOTE: **Importing Items That Are Already in the Database**

When you import your own music files, Spotify automatically checks to see if any of the tracks are in its own music database. If Spotify does have the track, it is made linkable to other devices and sharable with other users.

Summary

In this lesson, you learned how to import, play, and share local music files with your Spotify Local Files list. In the next lesson you learn about various ways to change your view of the music in your Spotify library.

LESSON 8

Viewing Your Music Library

In this lesson, you learn various ways in which you can change the view of the music in your Spotify library.

Understanding the Library

The first link in the Collection section of Spotify's navigation pane is for the Library. This is not Spotify's library, but rather *your* library. This is where Spotify lists your personal music, including the following:

- ▶ Playlists you've created or listened to

- ▶ Favorite tracks you've "starred"

- ▶ Any music you've purchased from inside Spotify (European users only; the U.S. version of Spotify does not offer music for sale)

- ▶ Local tracks you've imported into Spotify

In short, the Library is the master collection of your favorite and personal music. It does not contain all 15 million tracks in Spotify's database—just those tracks and playlists you like best.

Viewing and Playing Your Music

To view the Library, click Library in the Collection section of Spotify's navigation pane. As you can see in Figure 8.1, each track listed displays the following information in a series of columns, from left to right:

- ▶ Album cover artwork (click to display all tracks from this album)

- ▶ Star (for "starred" or favorite tracks)
- ▶ Share (click to share this track with others)
- ▶ Track number
- ▶ Track name
- ▶ Recording artist
- ▶ Time (length of track, in minutes and seconds)
- ▶ Album name

FIGURE 8.1   Viewing the Spotify library in album list view.

NOTE: **Resizing Columns**

To change the width of any column, position your cursor on the vertical line on the right side of that column header (the pointer changes to a double-headed arrow); then click and drag the edge of the column to the desired width. To automatically size a column to the width of its largest item, double-click the right side of that column's header.

To play a track, you can double-click the track or right-click the track and select Play from the pop-up menu. After you've started playback on one track, you can play another track by clicking it and then clicking the Play button in the transport controls.

Changing Library Views

By default, the Library is displayed in album list view—that is, all tracks are grouped by album and the album cover is displayed. To view the library as a straight list without album cover artwork, as shown in Figure 8.2, pull down the View menu and uncheck the View as Album List item. Re-check this item to display in album view again.

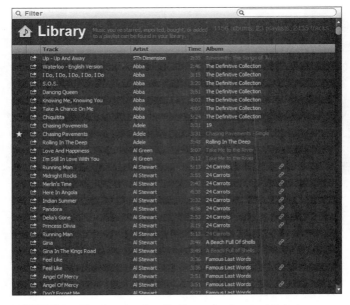

FIGURE 8.2   Viewing the Spotify library in standard list view.

Sorting the Library

By default, the Library is sorted by artist name and then by album name. (This is the first column in album view.) The default sort is in standard alphabetical order, A to Z. To reverse this sort order, click the header for the first column; this will change the order of the artist sort to Z to A.

You can sort the Library by any column, however, by clicking the appropriate column header, as shown in Figure 8.3. For example, to sort by track name, click the top of the Track column. To sort by album name, click the top of the Album column. And to sort by starred items, click the top of the "star" column. (To sort a column in reverse order, just click the top of the column a second time, so that the sort arrow points down instead of up.)

FIGURE 8.3   Sort your Library by clicking the appropriate column header.

NOTE: **First Name Sort**

Unfortunately, Spotify's sort function isn't that smart. It sorts artists by first name, instead of last. It does, however, ignore the words "The," "A," and "An."

Filtering Tracks

If you have a lot of tracks in your Spotify Library, you might want to filter what's displayed to find specific types of tracks. You do this from the Filter bar at the top of the Library page, shown in Figure 8.4.

FIGURE 8.4 Filtering Library contents from the Filter bar.

To filter your Library's contents, simply begin typing into the Filter box. As you type, only those contents that match what you type will be displayed. You don't have to press the Enter key when done.

For example, to display only tracks, artists, and albums that contain the word "water," type **water** into the Filter box. This will display tracks such as "Waterloo" and albums such as *Madman Across the Water*. Type **wonder** and Spotify displays tracks such as "'S Wonderful," artists like Stevie Wonder, and albums such as *New Magnetic Wonder*.

To clear a filter, click the X on the right side of the Filter box.

Summary

In this lesson, you learned how to control the view of the tracks stored in your Spotify Library. In the next lesson you learn how to search for music across the entire Spotify service.

LESSON 9

Searching for Music

In this lesson, you learn how to find music on the Spotify service using basic and advanced search parameters to locate a specific artist, album, or song.

Conducting a Basic Search

With 15 million tracks in its database, finding the music you want on Spotify can be daunting. Fortunately, Spotify makes it easy to search for music. You can search for

- ▶ Individual tracks

- ▶ Artists

- ▶ Playlists

You enter your search into the Search box at the top of the Spotify window. As you type, Spotify displays suggested matches in a drop-down list beneath the Search box, as shown in Figure 9.1. To select an item from the list, click it with your mouse. Otherwise, continue entering your query and then press the Enter key.

To clear the Search box, click the X on the right side of the box.

> NOTE: **Recent Searches**
> To view a drop-down list of recent searches, click the magnifying glass icon on the list.

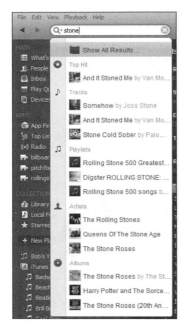

FIGURE 9.1   Searching for music.

Viewing Search Results

When you complete your search, Spotify displays a search results page like the one shown in Figure 9.2. There are four components to this page:

▶ **Playlists.** Displays the top playlists that include the word(s) you searched for in their titles.

▶ **Artists.** Displays those artists whose names include the word(s) you searched for.

▶ **Albums.** Displays those albums whose titles include the word(s) you searched for.

▶ **Tracks.** Displays tracks that match your query, or from artists or albums that match your query.

The Playlists, Artists, and Albums are displayed in three columns in the top half of the search results page. The tracks list comprises the bottom half of the page.

FIGURE 9.2   The results of a Spotify search.

Let's look at the top half of the results page first. Click the down arrow next to a column name to display additional items in that list. Click a playlist, artist name, or album title to display all tracks in that playlist, by that artist, or on that album.

When you click a playlist or album, you see a straight list of tracks included in that item. When you click an artist name, you see an artist page, which is covered in Lesson 11, "Viewing Artist Information."

The track list on the search results page includes all matching tracks, as well as tracks from matching artists and albums. The tracks listed include those in the master Spotify database, as well as those you've imported from your local computer. Local tracks are indicated by a music note icon to the right of the track listing.

NOTE: **Other Sorts**

Although the track list is sorted by popularity by default, you can sort by any other criteria by clicking that column header.

Songs in the track list are sorted in order of popularity among Spotify users—with the exception of your local tracks, which appear first in the list. If a track appears on more than one album, you see a down arrow next to the track title, as shown in Figure 9.3; click the down arrow to see all the albums where that track exists.

FIGURE 9.3   Click the down arrow to see all the albums that contain a given track.

To play a track, double-click the track name, click the track and then click the Play button in the transport controls, or right-click the track and select Play from the pop-up menu.

Conducting an Advanced Search

As you can see, Spotify's basic search can return a lot of useful results. However, you can fine-tune your searches with advanced search syntax, in order to return a shorter, more focused list of results.

Using Search Operators

One way to fine-tune your search is to use various *search operators*, terms or symbols that help to narrow the scope of a search. Table 9.1 details the search operators that Spotify allows.

Spotify's default search is the AND search—which means you don't have to use the AND operator. Include two or more words in a query and Spotify searches for results that include all of those words.

NOTE: **+ and -**

You can use the + operator in place of the AND operator to make sure a given word is included. You can also use the - operator instead of the NOT operator to make sure a given word is excluded from results.

TABLE 9.1   Spotify Search Operators

Operator	Description	Example
AND	Use to search for items that contain both words in a query.	**undun AND roots**—Finds the album *Undun* by The Roots.
OR	Use for an either/or search, to search for items that contain either one word or the other.	**undun OR roots**—Finds all artists who recorded the song "Undun," as well as all tracks by The Roots.
NOT	Use to exclude a word from search results.	**undun NOT roots**—Finds all artists who recorded the song "Undun" *except* for The Roots.

Searching for Specific Parameters

Spotify also offers a bevy of operators you can employ to restrict a search to specific parameters. You can use these operators to search for a specific track, artist, album, year, genre, or record label.

These parameters and their operators are detailed in Table 9.2. Enter the operator, followed by a colon (:) and then the word(s) you're searching for, with no space between the colon and the query.

TABLE 9.2   Continued

Parameter	Description	Example
artist	Finds artists matching the query.	**artist:beatles**
track	Finds song tracks matching the query.	**track:yesterday**
album	Finds albums matching the query.	**album:help**
year	Finds all music released during a particular year or period.	**year:1965** *or* **year:1980-1982**
genre	Finds all music in the specified genre.	**genre:jazz**
label	Finds all music released by the specified record label.	**label:EMI**

TABLE 9.2   Continued

Parameter	Description	Example
isrc	Displays the track that matches the ISRC (International Standard Recording Code) number.	**isrc:USGTH0600008**
upc	Displays the album that matches the uniform UPC (Universal Product Code) number.	**upc:074643243223**

NOTE: **Quotation Marks**

If a given parameter you're searching for contains more than one word, surround that phrase with quotation marks. For example, to search for the artist Katy Perry, enter **artist:"katy perry"**.

You can combine multiple parameters in a single query. For example, to search for all Americana music released in the 1990s, enter **genre:americana year:1990-1999**. To search for all Bruce Springsteen albums except for *Born to Run*, enter **artist:"bruce springsteen" NOT album:"born to run"** (and so on).

NOTE: **Genre List**

To view a list of all genres as identified by Spotify, go to www.spotify.com/us/about/features/advanced-search-syntax/genre-list/.

NOTE: **Search for New Albums**

Spotify offers one additional parameter, used with a single query. When you enter **tag:new**, Spotify lists the most recently added albums.

Summary

In this lesson, you learned how to search for music on the Spotify service. In the next lesson you learn how to play the music you find.

LESSON 10

Playing Tracks and Albums

In this lesson, you learn how to play music in Spotify.

Playing an Individual Track

Playing an individual song in Spotify is relatively easy. In fact, there are three ways to start playback of a given track:

▶ Double-click the track name.

▶ Right-click the track name and select Play from the pop-up menu.

▶ Select (single-click) the track name and then click the Play button in the transport controls. (This method works only after you've started playback of another track by another method.)

After you begin playing a track, you can control playback by using the transport controls at the bottom of the Spotify window, as shown in Figure 10.1. From left to right, these controls include the following:

FIGURE 10.1   Spotify's transport controls.

▶ **Rewind.** Click once to skip to the beginning of the current track, or click twice to return to the previous track.

▶ **Play/Pause.** Click once to pause playback. Click again to resume playback.

▶ **Fast forward.** Click to skip to the next track.

▶ **Volume.** Click and drag this slider to the left to lower the volume level, or to the right to play the music louder.

▶ **Seek.** This slider represents the current playback position within the track. The length of the track (in minutes and seconds) is displayed on the right side of this slider. You can click and drag the slider control to move playback to a new position.

▶ **Shuffle.** Click this button to randomly shuffle playback of selected tracks.

▶ **Repeat.** Click this button to keep repeating the current track.

The track you're currently playing is highlighted in the "now playing" area at the bottom of the navigation pane.

Playing an Album

Playing an entire album is just as easy as playing individual tracks. To play all the tracks from an album, simply navigate to the album, right-click the album's name or cover, and select Play.

NOTE: **No Shuffle**
To play an album's tracks in the original order, deactivate Spotify's shuffle mode by clicking "off" the Shuffle button at the lower-right corner of the application window.

Alternatively, you can double-click the album name or cover to open the album page, such as the one shown in Figure 10.2. From here you initiate playback by right-clicking the album cover and selecting Play. (If you double-click a single track within an album list, only that track plays.)

NOTE: **Album Reviews**
Many classic albums feature an in-depth review of the recording, like the one shown in Figure 10.2. Most newer albums do not.

FIGURE 10.2   Viewing an album page.

Playing Music in a Queue

You can play one track at a time, or select multiple tracks to add to a temporary playback *queue*. All tracks you add to a queue are played in order of when they were added—unless you're in shuffle mode, of course, when tracks are played in random order.

To add one or more tracks to a queue, select those tracks; then right-click and select Queue from the pop-up menu. (Select multiple tracks by holding down the Ctrl key while clicking each track.) To view your current queue, select Play Queue in the Main section of the navigation pane.

NOTE: **Drag and Drop**
You can also add tracks to your queue by dragging and dropping. Just drag a track or album from any list with Spotify (including your Library) and drop it onto the Play Queue item in the navigation bar. That track or album will now be added to your queue.

As you can see in Figure 10.3, all the tracks you've queued up are listed on the Play Queue page. Queued tracks will play immediately following the currently playing track; after all tracks in the queue are done playing, playback of the currently selected album or track resumes.

	Track	Artist	Time	Popularity	Album
Play Queue History					6 tracks queued
Playing from:					
●	Can You Feel It?	The Apples In Stereo	4:10	▋▋▋	New Magnetic Wonder
●	Jingle Jangle	The Archies	2:42	▋▋▋▋▋	Absolutely The Best Of The...
●	All I Know	Art Garfunkel	3:44	▋▋▋	Angel Clare
●	Say It (Over and Over Again)	Kurt Elling	6:40	▋▋▋	Dedicated To You: Kurt Elli...
●	Rock And Roll Crook	Nils Lofgren	2:56	▋	Ultimate Collection: Nils Lo...
○	Dun	The Roots	1:17	▋▋▋▋▋▋	Undun

FIGURE 10.3   Viewing your play queue.

Controlling Spotify from the Windows Taskbar

You don't have to leave the Spotify window open on your desktop to play your music. If you're a Windows user (version 7 and higher), you can access playback controls from the Windows task bar after you've minimized the Spotify window.

Just hover your mouse over the Spotify item in the taskbar. This displays the thumbnail and controls shown in Figure 10.4. From here you can pause, play, rewind, or fast forward music in your queue.

FIGURE 10.4   Controlling Spotify from the Windows taskbar.

Summary

In this lesson, you learned how to play music from within Spotify. In the next lesson you learn how to view information about recording artists.

LESSON 11

Viewing Artist Information

In this lesson, you learn how to view information about your favorite recording artists.

Finding Artists on Spotify

Recording artists are all over Spotify. Every track you play, every album you open, has at least one artist associated with it.

For example, all the tracks in your Library have an associated Artist column. Every track in a playlist has a similar Artist column. Even the Tracks and Albums lists on the Top Lists page have artists associated with each track or album.

You can also search Spotify for specific artists. Just enter the artist's name into the search box at the top of the Spotify window and then select the artist from the resulting drop-down list.

To view more information about a given artist, all you have to do is click the artist's name, wherever it appears on Spotify. This displays the artist page, which we discuss next.

Viewing Artist Information

There are three tabs on each artist page, located at the very top of the page:

> ► **Overview.** This tab displays a summary of the artist's bio, a handful of related artists, the artist's top hits, and all the albums that the artist has recorded or appeared on.

> ► **Biography.** This tab displays a detailed biography of the artist.

▶ **Related Artists.** This tab displays other artists similar to this one
that you might find interesting.

Let's start our journey with the Overview tab, which is divided into several
sections.

At the top of the Overview tab is some summary information about the
artist, as shown in Figure 11.1. You typically see a picture of the artist, a
list of which decades the artist was/is active, the first few lines of the
artist's biography, a handful of related artists (click an artist to display that
artist's Spotify page), a link to share that artist with other users, and a link
to start that artist's Spotify radio station.

FIGURE 11.1   Viewing an artist's overview information.

Next up is the Top Hits section, shown in Figure 11.2. This is a short list
of the artist's top five hits. You can star, share, or play any of these tracks
directly.

FIGURE 11.2   Viewing an artist's top hits.

Beneath this is the Albums section of the page, shown in Figure 11.3,
which lists (in reverse chronological order) all the albums this artist has
recorded under his or her own name. All the tracks for each album are also
listed. You can play an entire album by clicking the album cover and

FIGURE 11.3   Viewing the albums an artist has recorded.

selecting Play from the pop-up menu, or play an individual track by double-clicking it.

What appears next depends on the artist. For those artists who have released "singles" in addition to their album work, you see a Singles section, with each individual track listed. If an artist's work has appeared on any boxed sets or compilation albums, you'll see a Compilations section. And for those artists who have made guest appearances on other artists' albums, you see an Appears On section, with the tracks this artist played on listed for each album.

Reading the Artist Biography

To learn more about an artist's history, select the Biography tab on the artist page. This displays a detailed biography, like the one shown in Figure 11.4.

Brian Wilson

Brian Wilson is arguably the greatest American composer of popular music in the rock era. Born and raised in Hawthorne, CA, he formed the Beach Boys in 1961 alongside his two younger brothers, cousin Mike Love, and school friend Alan Jardine. Serving as the group's primary songwriter, Wilson combined the rock urgency of Chuck Berry with the harmonies of the Four Freshmen before expanding his musical imagination during the late '60s, during which time he experimented with new songwriting structures and production techniques. Wilson retreated from his dominance of the Beach Boys after 1967, yielding most of the control to his younger brother Carl. He made sporadic contributions to their records, returning only briefly as a songwriter and producer in the mid-'70s.

Following a long period of drug addiction, mental illness, and general isolation, Wilson issued his first solo album in 1988. Despite the promising lead single "Love and Mercy," commercial success proved elusive; ironically, the Beach Boys had recorded their own comeback record around the same time and wound up topping the charts with "Kokomo." Wilson attempted to find his footing with a second solo album, Sweet Insanity, which was rejected outright by Sire and permanently shelved. In 1995,

FIGURE 11.4   Viewing an artist's biography.

NOTE: **Links**

Many artist biographies include links to their albums on Spotify, or to other artists mentioned in the bio. Click one of these blue links to display that album or artist page.

Discovering Related Artists

Finally, you might be interested in other artists that sound similar to this artist or are related in some other way, such as being classified in the same genre. If so, select the Related Artists tab. As you can see in Figure 11.5, this page displays a barrage of artists who are in some ways similar to the original artist. Click an artist's thumbnail picture to display his or her Spotify artist page.

FIGURE 11.5 Displaying a related artist's page.

Summary

In this lesson, you learned how to find more information about a given recording artist. In the next lesson you learn how to play Spotify radio.

LESSON 12

Playing Spotify Radio

In this lesson, you learn how to create and play Spotify radio stations.

Understanding Spotify Radio

Spotify Radio is a special app built into the Spotify service. It lets you create virtual radio stations based on a single track or artist. These radio stations include music similar to the track or artist you selected—including other music by the original artist. The station's music streams to your computer over the Internet, and you can easily skip from track to track as you listen.

Spotify creates radio stations based on its intelligent recommendation engine. It uses what it knows about a given track and artist to identify other similar music, and adds those tracks to the station. You'll probably hear a lot of artists you've never listened to before—which makes Spotify Radio a great way to discover new music.

When you play a Spotify Radio station, it just keeps playing (until you pause the playback, of course); unlike a Spotify playlist, a station's track resources are virtually limitless. You can also easily go back and revisit any recent radio station you've created, just as you would a traditional radio station.

NOTE: **New Radio**
The new Spotify Radio is slightly different from Spotify's original Artist Radio. The new Spotify Radio lets all users, including those on the Free plan, play an unlimited number of tracks for a station, as well as skip an unlimited number of times. The original Artist Radio was more limited in its playback functionality.

Creating a New Radio Station

There are a number of different ways to create a new Spotify Radio station. Here are a few:

▶ Drag a track from any Spotify listing, such as your Library, onto the Radio item in the Apps section of Spotify's navigation pane.

▶ Go to any track listing, right-click a given track, then select Start Radio.

▶ Go to any artist page and click the Start Artist Radio link at the top of the page, as shown in Figure 12.1.

FIGURE 12.1   Creating a new radio station from an artist page.

▶ Click Radio in the Apps section of Spotify's navigation pane. When the Radio page appears, click the Create a New Station button. When the search pane appears, as shown in Figure 12.2, enter the name of an artist or song, then select the matching track or artist from the pull-down list.

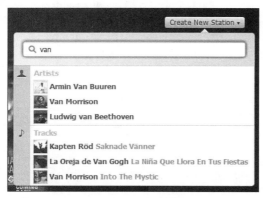

FIGURE 12.2   Creating a new radio station from the Spotify Radio page.

That's it. The new radio station is now created and displayed on Spotify's Radio page, as we discuss next.

Playing a Spotify Radio Station

When you create a new radio station, playback starts automatically. To view the current station, click Radio from the Apps section of the navigation pane. As you can see in Figure 12.3, the currently playing track is displayed underneath the album art at the top of this page. You can pause playback by hovering over the album artwork and clicking the Pause button; hover and click the Play button to resume playback.

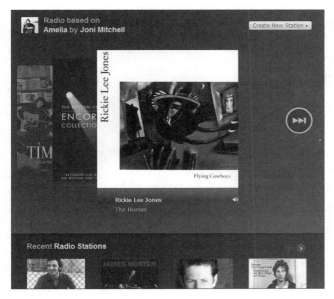

FIGURE 12.3   Listening to a Spotify Radio station.

Artist and track information is displayed beneath the now playing artwork. To skip to the next radio track, click the fast forward button to the right of the album artwork.

NOTE: **You Can't Go Back**
At present there is no way to move backward through the previously
played tracks of a radio station.

At the bottom of the radio page is a list of the recent radio stations you've
listened to. Click any given station thumbnail to begin listening to that station; click the right arrow at the top right of the stations list to view more
stations you've created or selected.

Summary

In this lesson, you learned how to create and listen to Spotify Radio stations. In the next lesson you learn how to identify and listen to your
favorite music on Spotify.

LESSON 13

Identifying and Playing Favorites

In this lesson, you learn how to "star" your favorite music on Spotify.

Understanding Stars

Spotify has a lot of stars—and we're not just talking famous performers. Your favorite music can also be "starred," so that Spotify knows what you like.

When you "star" a track, Spotify recognizes it as one of your favorites. It then organizes all your starred tracks in one location, so you can quickly and easily view and play your favorite music.

> NOTE: **Tracks and Albums**
> You can star both individual tracks and complete albums.

Starring Your Favorite Music

It's easy to tell Spotify which music is your favorite. Follow these steps:

1. From anywhere in Spotify, navigate to a track you like.

2. Click the empty star shape to the left of the track name, like the one shown in Figure 13.1.

FIGURE 13.1 A starred track (top) and an unstarred one (bottom).

The track is now "starred." A yellow star icon appears to the left of the track name wherever it is listed in Spotify. To "unstar" a track, simply click the yellow star again.

Viewing Starred Tracks

Starred tracks are visible in any Spotify list in which they would normally appear. To view all your starred tracks in a single list, go to the Collection section of the navigation pane and click Starred. This displays the Starred list, shown in Figure 13.2.

You play a starred track the same way you play any track, by double-clicking it within the list.

FIGURE 13.2   Viewing all your starred tracks.

TIP: **Share Starred Tracks in a Playlist**

You can share all your starred tracks with friends by creating a playlist consisting solely of starred tracks. We explore playlists in Lesson 14, "Creating and Playing Playlists."

Summary

In this lesson, you learned how to "star" your favorite music. In the next lesson you learn how to create and play playlists.

LESSON 14

Creating and Playing Playlists

In this lesson, you learn how to create and play playlists.

Understanding Playlists

In the last lesson you learned how to "star" your favorite music in Spotify. Another way to organize your favorite tracks is to put them into *playlists*.

A playlist is a collection of tracks grouped together for easy playback. You can create playlists around any topic you think of, or just put together a bunch of songs of any type that you like.

A Spotify playlist can include up to 10,000 individual tracks. Playlists can include tracks from multiple artists and albums, or can be constructed from tracks from a single artist.

After you create a playlist, it is listed in the Collection section of Spotify's navigation pane. You can easily play back an entire playlist in the track order listed or—when you shuffle the tracks—in random order.

Creating a New Playlist

To create a new playlist, follow these steps:

1. Go to the Collection section of Spotify's navigation pane.

2. Click the New Playlist item.

3. This creates a new unnamed playlist (labeled "New Playlist") at the top of the playlist list, as shown in Figure 14.1. Type a name for the playlist into the New Playlist text box and then press Enter.

FIGURE 14.1   Creating a new playlist.

There are several other ways to create a new playlist:

▶ Select File > New Playlist from the menu bar

▶ Press Ctrl+N on your computer keyboard

▶ Right-click a given track and select New Playlist from the pop-up menu

However you do it, you've created a new, empty playlist. You can now add tracks to the playlist, as described next.

> NOTE: **Collaborative Playlists**
> Spotify lets you create collaborative playlists, to which you and selected friends can add tracks. Learn more in Lesson 18, "Sharing and Collaborating on Playlists."

Adding Tracks to a Playlist

There are two ways to add new tracks to a playlist:

▶ Navigate to a track you want to add and then use your mouse to drag and drop that track onto the name of the playlist in the navigation pane.

▶ Navigate to and right-click a track you want to add. When the pop-up menu appears, select Add To and the name of the playlist.

Using either method, you can add multiple tracks at once by selecting more than one track first. To select consecutive tracks, hold down the Shift key while clicking; to select nonconsecutive tracks, hold down the Ctrl key while clicking. You can then right-click or drag the selected tracks to create the playlist.

Editing a Playlist

There are several ways you can edit an existing playlist. You can change track order, delete tracks, rename the playlist, or delete the entire playlist.

Changing the Order of Tracks

By default, tracks in a playlist are listed in order of when they were added to the playlist. You can, however, reorder the tracks in a playlist. To move a track within a playlist, simply use your mouse to drag and drop that track to a different position in the list.

You can also sort the tracks in a playlist by any primary criteria—track name, artist, length (time), or album name. Just click the header for the column you want to sort by.

Removing a Track

To remove a track from the playlist, right-click the track you want to delete and then select Delete. Note that this only deletes the track from the playlist, not from Spotify or your computer.

Renaming a Playlist

To rename the playlist, right-click the playlist in the navigation pane and select Rename from the pop-up menu. This opens the playlist title in a text box; edit or enter a new title into the box.

Deleting a Playlist

To delete an entire playlist, right-click the playlist in the navigation pane and select Delete from the pop-up menu. When prompted to confirm, as shown in Figure 14.2, click the red Delete button.

FIGURE 14.2   Deleting a playlist.

Note that this deletes the playlist but not the individual tracks, which remain in your Spotify library.

Grouping Playlists into Folders

If you've created a lot of playlists, you can organize them into different folders. This way you can group similar playlists together, and access them from a common folder. For example, you could create a Jazz folder to hold Cool Jazz, Bebop, and Big Band playlists. Or you might want to create an 80s folder and within it add playlists for Hair Bands, New Wave, and Hip Hop.

To create and use a playlist folder, follow these steps:

1. Select File > New Playlist Folder from the menu bar.

2. A "New Folder" item is added to the playlist section of the navigation pane. Click this item and enter a title for the folder.

3. To move a playlist to this folder, drag and drop the playlist name onto the folder name in the navigation bar.

When you select the playlist folder in the navigation bar, you see all the tracks from all the playlists in the folder. To view tracks for a specific playlist, open the folder in the navigation sidebar and select the individual playlist, as shown in Figure 14.3.

FIGURE 14.3   Displaying the playlists grouped into a folder.

Playing Back a Playlist

There are two ways to play back a playlist:

▶ Right-click the playlist name in the navigation pane and click Play from the pop-up menu

▶ Double-click the playlist name in the navigation pane

With either approach, the playlist opens in the main content pane, as shown in Figure 14.4, and begins playback. The currently playing track is indicated with a green speaker icon to the left of the track name. The number of tracks and total playing time of the playlist is displayed at the top of the pane, next to the playlist name.

FIGURE 14.4   Viewing a playlist page.

To pause playback, click the Play/Pause button. To resume playback, click the button again. To advance to the next track in the playlist, click the Fast Forward button. To play back the current track from the beginning, click the Rewind button once. To return to the previously played track, click the Rewind button twice.

While playing back a playlist, you can play the tracks in the original order added, or you can shuffle the playback—that is, play the tracks of the playlist in random order. To shuffle the playback, click the Shuffle button at the lower-right corner of the Spotify window.

Summary

In this lesson, you learned how to create and play playlists. In the next lesson you learn how to play your playlists when you're not connected to the Internet.

LESSON 15
Playing Music Offline

In this lesson, you learn how to use Spotify in Offline mode, without an Internet connection.

Understanding Offline Mode

Spotify is a streaming music service, which means that it feeds music over the Internet, in real time, to your computer or portable device. But what do you do if you don't have an Internet connection and still want to listen to music?

Good news—if you're a Premium or Ultimate subscriber, Spotify offers a special Offline mode, which works when you can't connect or don't want to be connected to the Internet (perhaps to save your device's battery charge, as discussed in Lesson 23, "Playing Spotify on Your iPhone"). You decide in advance which playlists you want to listen to while you're offline, and then those tracks are downloaded to your computer in advance. The next time your Internet connection is disconnected, Offline mode lets you play those playlists from within Spotify.

> NOTE: **No Free Offline**
> Offline mode is not available for Free subscriptions.

As you can imagine, this is especially helpful when you know you're going to be without an Internet connection for some time. For example, Offline mode lets you listen to your favorite playlists when you're on an airplane or traveling in your car.

Spotify's Offline mode works with playlists only, not individual tracks. You can sync your Offline playlists for up to three devices at once—for example, your notebook computer, iPad, and iPhone. Spotify lets you sync a maximum of 3,333 individual tracks for Offline listening.

Making a Playlist Available for Offline Listening

You need to activate Offline mode for each playlist you want to listen to while offline. Here's how you do it:

1. Click the playlist name in the navigation pane to open the playlist.

2. At the top of the playlist page, as shown in Figure 15.1, click the Available Offline switch to the right, so that the green "available" icon is displayed.

FIGURE 15.1   Activating Offline playback for a playlist.

Click the switch to the left to remove the playlist from Offline mode.

NOTE: **Right-Click to Use the Menu**
Alternatively, you can right-click the name of the playlist in the navigation pane and check Available Offline from the pop-up menu.

Listening Offline

To listen to your selected playlists offline, you don't have to do a thing—other than sever your Internet connection, that is. When your computer isn't connected to the Internet and you open Spotify, it launches in Offline mode. This is indicated by an icon in the lower-right corner of the window, as shown in Figure 15.2.

FIGURE 15.2   Spotify in Offline mode.

Playlists activated for Offline playback are indicated with a green down
arrow icon, as shown in Figure 15.3. You can play the tracks in these
playlists as you would normally. All other music is grayed out, and cannot
be played until you reestablish an Internet connection—unless the music is
locally stored, of course.

Spotify returns to normal mode when you re-establish your Internet connection.

FIGURE 15.3   A playlist available in Offline mode.

Summary

In this lesson, you learned how to use Spotify's Offline mode. In the next
lesson you learn how to connect your Facebook account (and friends) to
Spotify.

LESSON 16

Adding Your Friends to Spotify

In this lesson, you learn how to assemble a Spotify friends list.

Understanding Spotify Social

Spotify is more than just a music streaming service, it's a *social* music streaming service. That means you easily share the music you listen to with your friends—and they can share their music with you.

You can share music with other Spotify members, and with anyone on your Facebook friends list. (Remember, you signed into Spotify with your Facebook ID and password; this links your Spotify and Facebook accounts.) You can even post your Spotify tracks as Facebook status updates.

The key to social sharing is the concept of *friends.* You already know about Facebook's friends list; to share your favorite music, you need to assemble a similar list of your Spotify friends—what Spotify calls a *People list.* Your Spotify People list can include any other Spotify member, as well as anyone on your existing Facebook friends list.

Spotify displays your People list in the top half of the left-hand people pane, as shown in Figure 16.1. Sharing with a Spotify friend then becomes as easy as dragging a track to a name in the People list.

FIGURE 16.1   Spotify's People list.

Adding Facebook Friends

Let's start by examining how you can add your Facebook friends to your Spotify People list. Assuming that you've signed into Spotify with your Facebook ID, and thus linked your Spotify and Facebook accounts, it's a relatively easy process.

Here's how to add your Facebook friends to your Spotify People list:

1. Go to the Main section of the navigation pane and click People.

2. This displays your entire Facebook friends list in the center content pane, as shown in Figure 16.2. To display only those friends who are already subscribing to Spotify, click On Spotify at the top of the pane.

3. Hover over the thumbnail picture for the person you want to add and click the Add to Favorites button. Alternatively, you can drag and drop that person's thumbnail onto the People list, or right-click the thumbnail and select Add to Favorites.

The selected friend is now added to your People list. To remove a person from your People list, right-click that person's name and select Remove from Favorites from the pop-up menu, or hover over the thumbnail and click the Remove Favorite button.

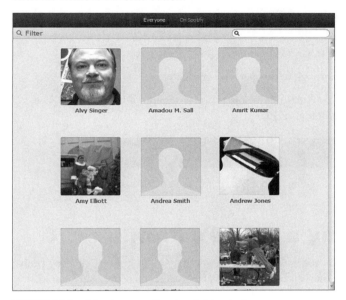

FIGURE 16.2   Viewing your Facebook friends list.

NOTE: **What About Non-Spotify Members?**
While you can add any Facebook friend to your Spotify People list, only those that are already Spotify members will receive the music you share.

Adding Other Spotify Users

You can also add any other Spotify user to your People list. To do so, however, you need to know the person's Spotify user ID or otherwise locate them on the Spotify site; at present, there is no way to search Spotify's master user list.

> NOTE: **Searching by Username**
>
> If you know the person's username, you can go directly to his or her profile page by entering **spotify:user:*username*** into the main search box.

To add a user to your People list, follow these steps:

1. Click through to this person's profile page.

2. Click the Add to Favorites button at the top of the profile page, as shown in Figure 16.3.

FIGURE 16.3   Adding a Spotify user to the People list.

Viewing a Friend's Profile

Whenever you see a user's name in Spotify, you're just a click away from viewing that user's profile. All you have to do is click the user's name, wherever it appears in Spotify. (For example, you'll see users' names in your People list, attached to any playlist or track they send you, and in the Trending Playlists and Top Tracks sections of Spotify's What's New page.)

When you click a user's name, you display his or her profile page in the middle content pane. (If this person isn't yet on your people list, you can add them at this point.) As you can see in Figure 16.4, a typical profile page includes the following content:

▶ User's picture (if one has been supplied)

▶ Last track listened to by this user (directly under the username at the top of the pane)

▶ Boxes to send this user a track or message

▶ Top Artists listened to by this user

▶ Playlists published by this user

FIGURE 16.4   Viewing a friend's Spotify profile.

Click any artist to view that artist's Spotify page. Double-click any track to listen to it.

Summary

In this lesson, you learned how to add friends to your Spotify People list. In the next lesson you learn how to share your favorite music with your friends.

LESSON 17

Sharing Music with Your Friends

In this lesson, you learn how to share tracks, albums, and artists.

How Spotify Sharing Works

As a social music sharing service, Spotify makes it relatively easy to share music with your friends. You can share to the following:

- ▶ Facebook, to either individual friends or to your entire friends list via a status update

- ▶ Twitter, to anyone following you on the Twitter service

- ▶ Spotify, to anyone you've added to your Spotify People list

- ▶ Messenger, to any of your contacts using the Windows Live Messenger instant messaging (IM) service

You can share individual tracks, complete albums, or artists.

Sharing Tracks

Sharing an individual track is one of the easiest things to do. Follow these steps:

1. Navigate to the track you want to share.

2. Right-click the track and select Share To from the pop-up menu.

3. When the sharing pop-up appears, as shown in Figure 17.1, select the tab for the service you want to share with.

4. Follow the instructions for the specific sharing service, as described later in this chapter.

FIGURE 17.1   Getting ready to share.

You can also display the sharing pop-up by clicking the sharing icon next to a track. As you can see in Figure 17.2, this icon is displayed on most list pages.

FIGURE 17.2   Click the sharing icon to display the sharing pop-up.

Sharing Albums

Sharing an entire album is similar to sharing a track. Follow these steps:

1. Navigate to the album you want to share.

2. Right-click the album title or cover art and select Share To from the pop-up menu.

3. When the sharing pop-up appears, select the tab for the service you want to share with.

4. Follow the instructions for the specific sharing service, as described later in this chapter.

Sharing Artists

To share your favorite artists, follow these steps:

1. Navigate to a track or album from the selected artist, and click the artist name.

2. When the artist page appears, click Share at the top of the page, as shown in Figure 17.3.

3. When the sharing pop-up appears, select the tab for the service you want to share with.

FIGURE 17.3   Sharing an artist.

4. Follow the instructions for the specific sharing service, as described later in this chapter.

Sharing to Facebook

Because Spotify and Facebook are linked, the two services make it quite easy for you to share your Spotify music with Facebook users. In fact, there are a number of different ways to do this.

Sharing Selected Items

When you find a track, album, or artist you want to share with your Facebook friends, follow these steps:

1. Right-click the item you want to share and select Share To.

2. When the sharing pop-up appears, select the Facebook tab.

3. Enter the message you want to accompany this shared item.

4. Click the Share to Facebook button.

The track/album/artist you selected is now posted to Facebook, accompanied by the message you wrote. The post appears on your Facebook profile page and in your friends' news feeds, like the post shown in Figure 17.4.

Michael Miller
I love this tune...

Hasten Down The Wind
Warren Zevon
Spotify

Like · Comment · Get Spotify · 6 seconds ago via Spotify

FIGURE 17.4   Sharing a track on Facebook.

If a friend is already a Spotify member, he or she can click the Play button and listen to the track/album/artist from within Facebook. If he isn't a Spotify member, he can click the Get Spotify link to sign up for Spotify.

Sharing Everything You Listen To

After you link your Spotify and Facebook accounts, everything you listen to on Spotify is sent to Facebook automatically. These tracks are displayed in your Facebook ticker, that piece of real-time real estate displayed in the top-right corner of the Facebook News Feed page. The tracks you listen to also contribute to the Spotify gadget displayed on your Facebook profile or timeline page, as shown in Figure 17.5.

You don't have to do anything to have the music you listen to sent to Facebook in this fashion; it's automatic. You can, however, disable this feature if you feel that it's sharing a little too much.

To disable Spotify's automatic Facebook sharing, follow these steps:

1. From within Spotify, select Edit, Preferences.

2. When the Preferences page appears, go to the Activity Sharing section at the top of the page, shown in Figure 17.6.

3. Uncheck the Show What I Listen To on Facebook option.

If you later decide you want to share your music on Facebook, repeat these steps and recheck the Show What I Listen To on Facebook option.

FIGURE 17.5 Your monthly Spotify listening displayed on your Facebook profile timeline.

FIGURE 17.6 Configuring Spotify not to share your listening with Facebook.

Opening a Private Session

You can also open Spotify in a *private session*—that is, a listening session that is not automatically shared with Facebook. With this option selected, Spotify does not share any of the music you listen to for the duration of this listening session—that is, until you log into Spotify again or end your private session.

To open a private session, pull down the File menu and check the Private Session option. To exit a private session, uncheck the Private Session option.

Sharing to Twitter

If you have a Twitter account, you can share any selected track/album/artist as a tweet. Here's how to do it:

1. Right-click the item you want to share and select Share To.

2. When the sharing pop-up appears, select the Twitter tab.

3. As you can see in Figure 17.7, a link to the item is already entered into the text box, along with the #NowPlaying hashtag and a short message. You can accept this message as is or edit it as you wish.

FIGURE 17.7   Tweeting a track via Twitter.

4. Click the Share to Twitter button.

The link to this track/album/artist is now tweeted to your followers.

> NOTE: **What's a Hashtag?**
> On Twitter, a hashtag is a kind of keyword that other users can use to search for hot topics.

Sharing to Spotify

When you want to share a track/album/artist with a fellow Spotify member, you simply send a link to that item to that person's Spotify inbox. There are two ways to do this.

Sharing an Item

To send an item via drag-and-drop, follow these steps:

1. Navigate to the item you want to share; then use your mouse to drag and drop that item onto your friend's name in your People list.

2. When the message pop-up appears, as shown in Figure 17.8, enter a short message to accompany the link (optional).

3. Click the Send button.

FIGURE 17.8   Sharing to Spotify via drag-and-drop.

TIP: **Button Changes**

The label on the Send button varies to match the kind of item you're sharing: Send Album, Send Track, or Send Artist. For simplicity, I'll call it the Send button in these steps.

NOTE: **No Imported Tracks**

You can only send streaming items via drag-and-drop. You cannot use this method to send tracks imported from and stored on your computer.

Alternatively, you can follow these steps to share an item:

1. Right-click the item you want to share and select Share To.

2. When the sharing pop-up appears, select the Spotify tab.

3. Enter the person's name into the To box (see Figure 17.9); a list of matching names from friends in your People list appears. Select a name from this list.

4. Enter a short message (optional) to accompany the link.

5. Click the Send button.

FIGURE 17.9   Sharing to Spotify via right-clicking.

Listening to a Shared Item

All items shared with you are displayed in your Spotify inbox. To display your inbox, click Inbox in the Main section of the Spotify navigation pane.

As you can see in Figure 17.10, items you've not yet listened to are displayed with a blue dot to the left of the track name. To listen to an item, double-click it. To read a message accompanying an item, click the message balloon to the right of the sender's name.

FIGURE 17.10   Viewing shared items in your inbox.

Sharing to Windows Live Messenger

Finally, you can share tracks/albums/artists with any of your friends who happen to be on the Windows Live Messenger IM service. (This presumes, of course, that you also have a Windows Live Messenger account.)

To share music via instant messaging, follow these steps:

1. Right-click the item you want to share and select Share To.

2. When the sharing pop-up appears, select the Messenger tab (see Figure 17.11).

FIGURE 17.11   Getting ready to share via Windows Live Messenger.

3. Enter an accompanying message (optional).

4. Click the Share to Messenger button.

5. The Windows Live sign in page appears in your web browser. Enter your Windows Live ID and password and then click the Sign In button.

6. You now see the Share with Messenger page, as shown in Figure 17.12. Click Via an Instant Message at the top of the page.

7. Enter the name of the person you want to share with into the Search Contacts box and then select the desired contact from the resulting list.

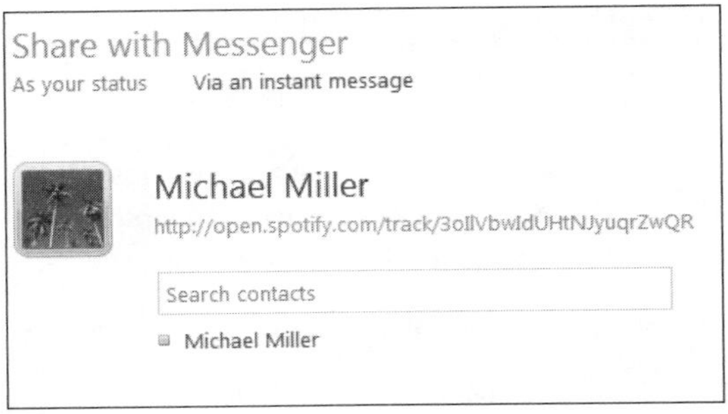

Share with Messenger
As your status   Via an instant message

Michael Miller
http://open.spotify.com/track/3oIlVbwIdUHtNJyuqrZwQR

Search contacts

☐ Michael Miller

FIGURE 17.12   Sharing via instant message.

8. An instant message session now begins, with your link to this track as your first message.

Sharing to Anyone on the Web

You can also share your Spotify music with anyone you communicate with on the Web. It's a simple matter of pasting a link to a track/album/artist into an email, blog post, or web page.

To share a web link to a Spotify item, follow these steps:

1. Navigate to and right-click the item you want to share.

2. Select Copy HTTP Link from the pop-up menu.

3. Paste the copied link into your email, blog post, or web page.

It's that simple. You can also paste this link into a Facebook or Google+ post, a Twitter tweet, a post to a web-based message forum, or any web-based communications medium.

Summary

In this lesson, you learned how to share your music with your friends. In the next lesson you learn how to share and collaborate on Spotify playlists.

LESSON 18

Sharing and Collaborating on Playlists

In this lesson, you learn how to share your Spotify playlists with friends and how to work with your friends to create and edit custom playlists.

Sharing a Playlist

In Lesson 17 you learned how to share tracks, albums, and artists. Sharing playlists works exactly the same way, except you're sharing all the tracks in a given playlist—or at least those tracks that stream from Spotify.

To share a playlist, follow these steps:

1. Right-click the playlist in the navigation pane and select Share To.

2. When the sharing pop-up appears, as shown in Figure 18.1, select the tab for how you want to share—Facebook, Twitter, Spotify, or Messenger.

3. Enter an accompanying message, if you like, and then click the Share or Send button.

FIGURE 18.1   Sharing a Spotify playlist.

Collaborating on a Playlist

A *collaborative playlist* is one that you not only share with others, but that others can also edit. You and your friends all see the same playlist in the Collection section of your Spotify navigation panes; when one person makes a change to the playlist, that change appears in everyone's version of the playlist, in real time.

Collaborative playlists let multiple music lovers team up to share their musical likes and dislikes. It turns music curation into a team sport and helps you build better playlists with the musical knowledge of others.

You can turn any playlist into a collaborative playlist. Follow these steps:

1. In the Collection section of the navigation pane, right-click the playlist you want to collaborate on and select Collaborative Playlist from the pop-up menu.

2. The music note icon to the left of the playlist name now turns green, with a little dot to the left (see Figure 18.2). Right-click the playlist and select Share To.

FIGURE 18.2   A collaborative playlist.

3. When the sharing pop-up appears, select the Spotify tab.

4. Enter the person's name you want to share with into the To box and then enter a message, if you like, into the Optional Message box.

5. Click the Send Playlist button.

Your friend now receives a message in her Spotify inbox. When she opens the message she sees the playlist page shown in Figure 18.3. To collaborate on the playlist, she needs to click Subscribe at the top of the playlist page.

FIGURE 18.3 Subscribing to a collaborative playlist.

After they've subscribed to the collaborative playlist, your friends can add tracks to and delete tracks from the playlist. Their changes appear on your playlist page as they make them, and your changes appear on their versions of the playlist.

> CAUTION: **Careful Collaboration**
> You can share a collaborative playlist with any number of people, but remember that anyone you share it with is able to alter the playlist and to invite others to collaborate, as well. For this reason, you should be careful about who you share your playlists with.

As the creator of the playlist, you can turn off playlist collaboration at any time. Just right-click the playlist and uncheck the Collaborative Playlist option. People you shared the playlist with are still able to view and listen to the playlist, but they won't be able to make any more changes.

> NOTE: **No Publishing**
> Unlike normal playlists, collaborative playlists are not published to your Spotify profile page.

Summary

In this lesson, you learned how to share and collaborate on playlists. In the next lesson you learn how to discover new music via Spotify's Top Lists.

LESSON 19

Viewing Top Lists

In this lesson, you learn how to view the top albums and tracks on Spotify.

Viewing Top Tracks and Albums

When it comes to discovering new music, nothing beats finding out what others are listening to. To that end, Spotify publishes two real-time "top music" lists that display the most popular songs and albums among Spotify users.

You display these top music lists by clicking the Top Lists item in the Apps section of Spotify's navigation pane. As you can see in Figure 19.1, there are two of these lists—Top Tracks and Top Albums. Each list displays the 100 most listened-to items by Spotify users.

FIGURE 19.1   Viewing Spotify's Top Lists page.

By default, the Top Lists page displays the top tracks and albums in the U.S. However, you can change this to display the top items in the entire world, in specific countries, or that you yourself have listened to. All you have to do is click the down arrow at the top of either list, as shown in Figure 19.2, and make a selection from the pull-down menu:

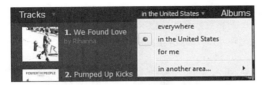

FIGURE 19.2   Changing the type of list to view.

▶ **Everywhere.** Lists the top tracks and albums from all Spotify users across the globe.

▶ **In the United States.** The default selection; lists top tracks and albums from U.S. listeners only.

▶ **For me.** Select this option to see the top tracks and albums you've listened to.

▶ **In another area.** Choose this option and then select from one of the following countries: Denmark, Spain, Finland, France, United Kingdom, Netherlands, Norway, Sweden, Austria, Switzerland, or Belgium.

You can also change the lists you view. By default you view top tracks and albums, but you can also opt to view the top artists on Spotify. To do this, click the down arrow next to either the Tracks or Albums header and select Artists. The list now changes to display the most listened-to artists, as shown in Figure 19.3.

Viewing Your Friends' Top Music

You may also be interested in the music that your friends are listening to. To that end, you can view your friends' top tracks and playlists, as well as the top tracks and playlists from your neighbors.

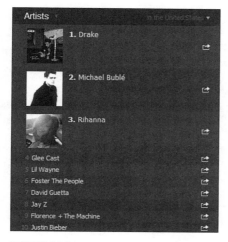

FIGURE 19.3   The Top Tracks list changed to a Top Artists list.

Begin by clicking What's New in the Main section of Spotify's navigation pane. When the What's New page appears, scroll past the recommended album display to the Trending Playlists Among Friends and Top Tracks Among Friends lists, shown in Figure 19.4. The first list contains your friends' most popular playlists (assuming you have enough friends who've created playlists, that is); click a playlist title to view the playlist page, complete with all the tracks in the playlist. The second list contains those tracks most listened to by your Spotify friends.

Trending playlists among friends		Top tracks among friends	
		Title	Artist
Superstar by Joe Wikert		☆ When I Fall In Love - featu...	Renee Olstead
TechTalk.wrlr.fm - Podcast Only Music by Michael Kastler		☆ The Way Away From You	The Ten Tenors
		☆ My Immortal - Band Version	Evanescence
Dan Fogelberg by Larry J White		☆ Bump In The Road	Jonny Lang
		☆ Christmas (Baby Please Co...	U2
		☆ Valerie - '68 Version	Amy Winehouse
		☆ Lights - Single Version	Ellie Goulding
		☆ Keep Pushin'	REO Speedwagon

FIGURE 19.4   Viewing your friends' top playlists and tracks.

To discover what your neighbors are listening to, scroll to the bottom of the What's New page to view the Top Playlists Near You and Top Tracks Near You lists, shown in Figure 19.5. These lists compile the most listened-to playlists and tracks from those Spotify users geographically near you. You never know—your neighbors might be secretly hip!

FIGURE 19.5   Viewing the most listened-to playlists and tracks from people near you.

Summary

In this lesson, you learned how to view lists of the most listened-to music on Spotify. In the next lesson you learn how to extend Spotify with apps.

LESSON 20

Exploring Spotify Apps

In this lesson, you learn how to enhance Spotify with various third-party apps.

Understanding Spotify Apps

An app is a small application designed for a specific purpose. Spotify has opened its underlying technology platform so that other companies can develop apps for use by Spotify members. You can add apps to your version of the Spotify software that provide enhanced value when you're using Spotify.

Maybe you'd like some tips on new music to listen to? There are apps for that. Maybe you'd like to see the lyrics for a particular song? There's an app for that. Or maybe you'd like to be notified when your favorite artists are performing live nearby? There's an app for that, too.

There are more than a dozen apps currently available for Spotify, with more to come. What they have in common is that they're designed to help you better enjoy the music you listen to on Spotify.

Oh, and they're free.

Finding and Installing Apps

To discover what Spotify apps are available, and to install the apps you want, follow these steps:

1. Go to the Apps section of Spotify's navigation pane and click App Finder.

2. This displays the App Finder page in the content pane, as shown in Figure 20.1. Navigate to any app you find interesting.

FIGURE 20.1   Discovering Spotify apps with the App Finder.

3. To learn more about a given app, click its title to see a dedicated page for that app, provided by the app's developer.

4. To install an app, click the blue Add button.

A link to that app is now added to the Apps section of the navigation sidebar.

> NOTE: **Uninstalling Apps**
> To uninstall an app from Spotify, right-click its link in the sidebar and select Remove from Sidebar from the pop-up menu.

Using Spotify Apps

To access an installed app, just go to the Apps section of Spotify's navigation sidebar. As you can see in Figure 20.2, all the apps you've installed are listed there. Click the name of the app you want to use, and that app is displayed in the main content pane.

FIGURE 20.2   Your installed apps, in Spotify's navigation pane.

> NOTE: **Sharing Apps**
>
> To share an app with another user, right-click the app's name in the sidebar and select Copy HTTP Link from the pop-up menu. You can now paste that link into an email message or Facebook update to share with friends.

Evaluating Popular Apps

What apps can you add to Spotify? As noted, there are more than a dozen currently available; we'll look at each individually.

Billboard Top Charts

What's the hottest music in the nation? *Billboard* has tracked the top hits for decades, and offers its most popular charts to Spotify users (see Figure 20.3). These charts include the Hot 100, Billboard 200, R&B/Hip-Hop Songs, Country Songs, and Rock Songs. For those songs that are available on Spotify, all you have to do is click a track to listen to it.

Fuse

Fuse provides the latest music industry news, complete with playlists tailored to each story reported. As you can see in Figure 20.4, it's great information at your fingertips—from within Spotify.

Last.fm

Last.fm is a complementary music service to Spotify that recommends new music you might like, based on your Spotify listening. Learn more in Lesson 21, "Scrobbling Your Music to Last.fm."

FIGURE 20.3   The Billboard Top Charts app.

FIGURE 20.4   The Fuse app.

Moodagent

Moodagent automatically creates new Spotify playlists based on those tracks you select. As you can see in Figure 20.5, you enter the name of a track, select the mood for the playlist (sensual, tender, happy, or angry), and let Moodagent assemble complementary music.

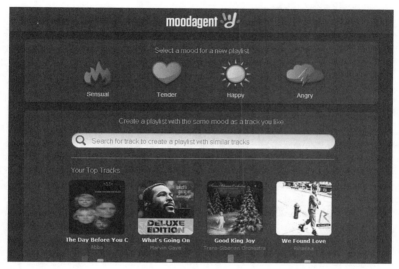

FIGURE 20.5   The Moodagent app.

Pitchfork

Pitchfork offers online music reviews of the latest releases. As you can see in Figure 20.6, you can easily add the albums reviewed by Pitchfork as Spotify playlists.

Rolling Stone Recommends

The legendary *Rolling Stone* magazine recommends a variety of playlists, albums, and individual songs for your listening pleasure. Figure 20.7 shows some of what *Rolling Stone* recommends.

FIGURE 20.6   The Pitchfork app.

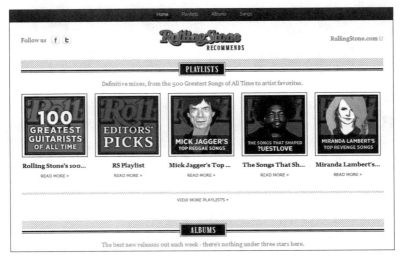

FIGURE 20.7   The Rolling Stone Recommends app.

ShareMyPlaylists

Use ShareMyPlaylists to, well, to share your playlists with others—and to share their playlists, too. As you can see in Figure 20.8, you can view and listen to playlists created by other users, as well as drag and drop your playlist into the app to share it with other ShareMyPlaylists users. There's even a unique playlist generator that lets you create a new playlist just by entering an artist's name.

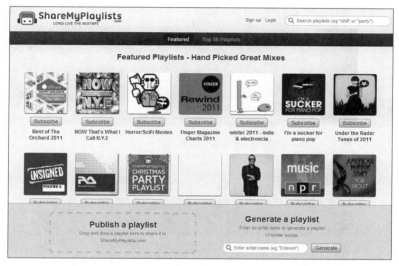

FIGURE 20.8   The ShareMyPlaylists app.

Songkick Concerts

Here's a good one. Songkick scans your Spotify library and playlists for your favorite artists, and then notifies you when they're performing nearby. Figure 20.9 shows you what it looks like.

Soundrop

Soundrop presents another way to share and listen to music with your friends. As you can see in Figure 20.10, you can enter or create your own online "listening rooms," which include real-time chat with other listeners.

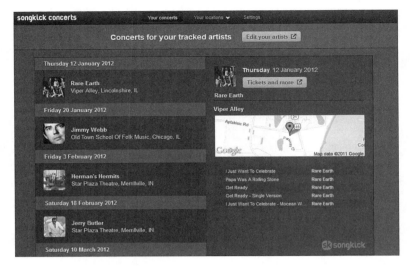

FIGURE 20.9   The Songkick Concerts app.

FIGURE 20.10   The Soundrop app.

Spotify Radio

This app is developed by and built into Spotify to generate real-time "radio stations" based on your favorite tracks or artists. Learn more in Lesson 12, "Playing Spotify Radio."

Spotify Top Lists

This is another built-in app, designed to show you Spotify's top artists, albums, and tracks. Learn more in Lesson 19, "Viewing Top Lists."

The Guardian

This app, shown in Figure 20.11, lets you read the latest album reviews from *The Guardian*, one of the U.K.'s top newspapers.

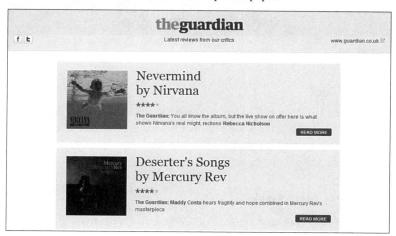

FIGURE 20.11   Spotify's The Guardian app.

Top10

Top10 is another playlist creation and sharing app. As you can see in Figure 20.12, this app lets you create playlists of your top 10 songs in various categories, as well as browse and listen to other users' top 10 playlists.

FIGURE 20.12   The Top10 app.

TuneWiki

Can't remember the lyrics to a given song? TuneWiki can help. All you have to do is start playing a song in Spotify then launch TuneWiki; as you can see in Figure 20.13, TuneWiki displays the song's lyrics onscreen, synced to the song's playback.

We Are Hunted

Want to discover hot new music? We Are Hunted exposes you to the latest tracks from emerging artists; you can also view new songs by genre and create new playlists based on existing artists you like. Figure 20.14 shows what it looks like.

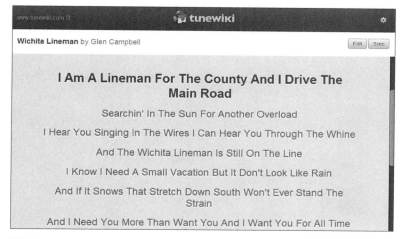

FIGURE 20.13 The TuneWiki app.

FIGURE 20.14 The We Are Hunted app.

Summary

In this lesson, you learned how to find and use Spotify apps. In the next lesson you learn how to use one of these apps, Last.fm.

LESSON 21

Scrobbling Your Music to Last.fm

In this lesson, you learn how to use Spotify with Last.fm.

Understanding Last.fm

As you know, Spotify is a streaming music service that makes it easy to listen to music wherever there's an Internet connection. Although Spotify is great for finding and playing the music you know and love, it's less useful for discovering new music.

Enter Last.fm. Last.fm is a UK-based website designed solely to introduce listeners to new music, based on their current musical tastes. The site works in conjunction with various media players and streaming music services, such as Spotify; you send Last.fm the music you listen to and it evaluates your musical tastes and recommends other music you might like.

Last.fm calls this transmittal of music from one service to another *scrobbling*. Its "Audioscrobbler" music recommendation system creates a detailed profile of each user's musical tastes and then matches that user to other similar music in its database of tracks.

What you get in return is a slew of recommendations in terms of other artists and albums you might like. As you can see in Figure 21.1, Last.fm also creates your own personal online radio station.

Like Spotify's basic service, Last.fm is free. You can learn more at the www.last.fm website.

FIGURE 21.1   Viewing your personal recommendations on the Last.fm website.

Scrobbling to Last.fm

For Last.fm to analyze your musical tastes and make its recommendations, it has to know what music you're listening to. Spotify makes this easy by automating the scrobbling process—in effect, notifying Last.fm of all the tracks you listen to.

To activate Last.fm scrobbling within Spotify, you must first go to Last.fm and create an account. (It's free.) You then return to Spotify and follow these steps:

1. Select Edit, Preferences.

2. When the Preferences page appears, go to the Activity Sharing section at the top of the page, shown in Figure 21.2.

FIGURE 21.2 Enabling scrobbling from within Spotify.

3. Check the Scrobble to Last.fm option.

4. If prompted, enter your Last.fm username and password into the Username and Password boxes.

Spotify now sends information about each track you play to Last.fm. You can then visit the Last.fm site to view your personalized recommendations—or use the Last.fm app within Spotify to the same effect.

Using Spotify's Last.fm App

The previous lesson covered how you can use third-party apps to add functionality to Spotify. One of the most popular apps is the Last.fm app, which lets you see the personalized recommendations resulting from your scrobbling—and use those recommendations to play new music on Spotify.

To use the Last.fm app, you must first install it from the Apps List page. To launch the app, click Last.fm in the Apps section of the navigation pane.

NOTE: **Logging In**

The first time you open the Last.fm app you're prompted to either log into your existing Last.fm account or create a new account. Do whichever is necessary to proceed.

The Last.fm app consists of four tabs, clickable at the top of the page—Overview, Now Playing, Recommended, and Albums. We'll look at each individually.

Overview

Use the Overview tab, shown in Figure 21.3, to get a quick glance at Last.fm's recommendations. Here you find the following:

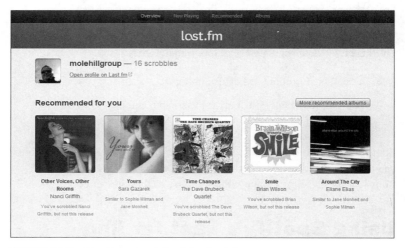

FIGURE 21.3   The Overview tab of the Last.fm app.

▶ Your username and profile picture (if any). To view your full Last.fm profile in your web browser, click the Open Profile on Last.fm link.

▶ The Recommended for You section lists Last.fm's top recommended albums, based on other music you've played.

▶ The Albums section displays those albums you've played within the past three months.

▶ The Recent Tracks section lists those individual tracks you've recently played on Spotify.

▶ The Loved Tracks section lists those tracks you've "loved" on Last.fm—similar to starred tracks on Spotify.

Now Playing

The Now Playing tab, shown in Figure 21.4, details the track you're currently listening to on Spotify. Not only do you see information about the track and recording artist, you can also "love" the track (click the Love Track button) or create a playlist with similar tracks (click the Similar Tracks Playlist button). Similar artists are listed beneath the track/artist description.

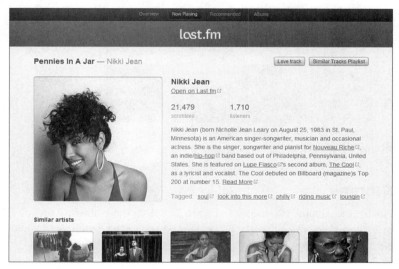

FIGURE 21.4   The Now Playing tab of the Last.fm app.

Recommended

The Recommended tab, shown in Figure 21.5, lists a dozen albums Last.fm recommends based on your current listening habits. Under each album cover, Last.fm describes why this album is recommended. Click an album to listen to it now.

To view more recommended albums, click the More button at the top of the page. To create a Spotify playlist from music on these albums, click the Add as Playlist button.

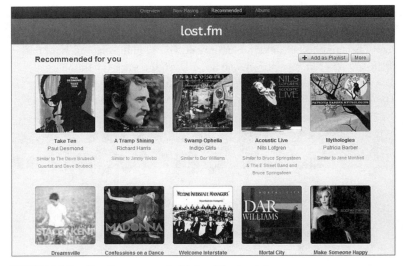

FIGURE 21.5   The Recommended tab of the Last.fm app.

Albums

Finally, the Albums tab, shown in Figure 21.6, lists those albums you've recently listened to on Spotify. Click the Add as Playlist button to add this album as a Spotify playlist.

> TIP: **Hidden Playlist Feature**
>
> Here's a hidden feature in the Last.fm app. When you drag a song from your Spotify library and drop it on the Last.fm title in the sidebar, Last.fm automatically creates a playlist of twenty tracks similar to that song!

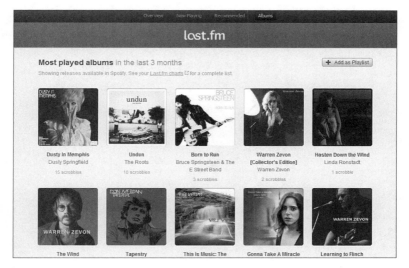

FIGURE 21.6 The Albums tab of the Last.fm app.

Summary

In this lesson, you learned how to use Last.fm together with Spotify to get new music recommendations. In the next lesson you learn how to sync Spotify with your iPod music player.

LESSON 22

Syncing Spotify to Your iPod

In this lesson, you learn how to sync your Spotify music with an iPod portable music player.

What You Can and Can't Sync

Spotify is a streaming music service, which means the music you listen to is streamed "live" across the Internet to your computer or wireless device. How, then, can you listen to Spotify on an iPod or other portable music player that doesn't have Internet access—one that plays music back from its own internal storage?

The solution is to sync your iPod with your Spotify account—that is, to transfer tracks from the Spotify library on your computer to your iPod. Now, you can't transfer tracks you've listened to via streaming, or those you might listen to in the future. What you can transfer, however, are those local tracks you previously imported into Spotify.

> NOTE: **Importing Tracks**
> To learn more about importing local tracks into Spotify, see Lesson 7, "Importing Your Local Music Files into Spotify."

Spotify enables you to transfer to your iPod or other portable music player those tracks stored on your computer that have been added to your Spotify library. The music files are manually synced, or copied, to your iPod from Spotify. You can then listen to these tracks—tracks you already own—on your portable music player.

> NOTE: **iPhones**
>
> The situation is different if you listen to your music on an iPhone or
> other devices with wireless Internet connectivity. Learn more in
> Lesson 23, "Playing Spotify on Your iPhone."

Syncing Your Music

When you sync your iPod or similar device, all music files you have
imported into Spotify (and stored in your Local Files folder) are trans-
ferred to your iPod.

> CAUTION: **Your Content Will Be Erased**
>
> When you sync tunes from Spotify to your iPod, much of the con-
> tent currently on your iPod is erased, including music, movies, TV
> shows, and audiobooks. Only photos and podcasts remain.

Transferring Music to Your iPod

To sync your iPod with Spotify, follow these steps:

1. Open Spotify on your computer.

2. Connect your iPod to your computer.

3. Your iPod appears in the Devices section of Spotify's navigation
   pane, as shown in Figure 22.1. Click the link for your iPod.

FIGURE 22.1   Your iPod in Spotify's navigation pane.

4. When the iPod page appears, as shown in Figure 22.2, click
   Erase iPod & Sync with Spotify.

FIGURE 22.2   Getting ready to sync your iPod.

Follow the onscreen instructions to complete the sync. After the transfer is complete, all your local Spotify tracks are available for playback on your iPod. Album art for each track also appears if your iPod displays album covers.

> NOTE: **Manual Selection**
> By default, Spotify syncs all the content in your Local Files library to your iPod. If you'd rather select which playlists to sync, click Manually Choose Playlists to Sync on the iPod page in Spotify.

Unsyncing Your iPod

If you want to stop syncing your iPod with Spotify and resume using iTunes, follow these steps:

1. Close Spotify on your computer and make sure your iPod is *not* connected to your computer.

2. Launch the iTunes software.

3. Connect your iPod to your computer.

4. Click your iPod in iTunes' Devices list.

5. Open the Music tab.

6. Click within the Sync Music checkbox.

7. When the message box appears, click Sync Music.

8. Click the Apply button.

9. When prompted, click Erase and Sync.

Your iPod is now re-synced with iTunes, and no longer synced with Spotify.

Summary

In this lesson, you learned how to sync your iPod with Spotify. In the next lesson you learn how to use Spotify on your iPhone.

Playing Spotify on Your iPhone

In this lesson, you learn how to play music from Spotify on your iPhone.

Understanding Spotify Mobile

If you subscribe to Spotify's Premium plan ($9.99/month), you can stream music from Spotify on your iPhone or other mobile device. You do this by installing the Spotify Mobile app for your device. Spotify has apps for the following smartphones and devices:

▶ iPhone and iPod touch

▶ Android

▶ Windows Phone

▶ Palm OS

▶ BlackBerry

▶ Symbian

You can find the Spotify Mobile app in your phone's app store, or learn more online at www.spotify.com/mobile/.

> NOTE: **Non-Premium Users**
> To fully enjoy Spotify streaming on your phone, you must subscribe to the Premium plan. Non-Premium subscribers, however, can still listen to local music files you import into Spotify by using the Spotify Mobile app; you just can't listen to any tracks you don't own.

For the purposes of this lesson we'll be examining the Spotify Mobile app for the Apple iPhone. You can download this app (for free) from the iPhone App Store. After you install the app on your iPhone, you need to launch it and log into your existing Spotify account when you're prompted.

> NOTE: **Connection Required**
> Naturally, your phone needs to be connected to the Internet, either via Wi-Fi or 3G, to access Spotify.

Viewing and Playing Playlists

The Spotify Mobile app has five tabs, accessible from the bottom of any screen—Playlists, Search, What's New, Friends, and Settings. When you want to listen to your favorite music, the Playlists tab is a good place to start.

As you can see in Figure 23.1, the Playlists tab lists all the playlists you've created in Spotify. It also includes your Starred list, your Inbox (music sent to you from your friends), and your Local files imported from your computer.

FIGURE 23.1   Spotify Mobile's Playlists tab.

NOTE: **Syncing Local Files**

Before you can view any local files you've imported on your mobile device, you have to sync your phone with your computer. To do this, both your computer and iPhone need to be connected to the same wireless network. Then go to the Playlists tab on your phone, tap Local, then turn the Available Offline switch to On for this folder to download your local music from your computer to your iPhone.

To view a playlist, simply tap its name. This displays the playlist screen, such as the one shown in Figure 23.2. To start playback in Shuffle mode, tap the Shuffle Play icon. Otherwise, tap the first track in the playlist to play the tracks in their assigned order.

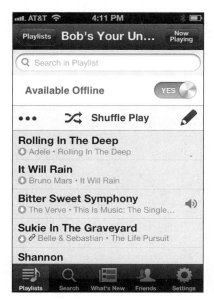

FIGURE 23.2   Viewing a playlist.

To change the order of the tracks in a playlist, tap the Edit (pencil) icon. You can then drag and drop any track to a new position within the playlist. You can also tap the Edit button and then tap the red button next to any track to delete it from the playlist. Tap the Edit button again to leave editing mode.

Other options are available if you tap the top left ellipsis (three dots) icon. You can then edit the playlist (same as with the Edit icon), share the playlist, or make a playlist collaborative.

Tap the Playlists button to return to the master Playlists page.

Playing Music

To view the currently playing track, tap the Now Playing button. This displays the album page for the track (Figure 23.3 shows an example). You see the image for the track as well as the main playback controls—Rewind, Pause/Play, and Fast Forward. The track scrubber for moving back and forth within a track is at the very bottom of the page.

FIGURE 23.3   The Now Playing page.

To view more information about this track, tap the Info (i) button at the top-left corner of the screen (see Figure 23.4). From here you can do the following:

▶ Tap the track name to view the album page that contains this track.

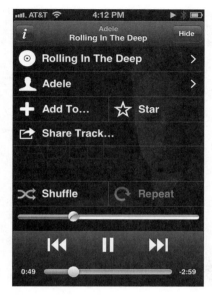

FIGURE 23.4   Viewing more track information.

▶ Tap the artist name to view the Spotify page for this artist, like the one shown in Figure 23.5. From here you can view and play additional albums, singles, and other tracks this artist appears on.

▶ To add this track to a playlist, tap Add To (+) and then select the playlist from the list.

▶ To "star" this as a favorite track, tap the Star icon.

▶ To share this track with a friend, tap Share Track. When the Share Track page appears, as shown in Figure 23.6, you can choose to email a link to this track; send the track to one or more people in your Spotify People list; share the track to Facebook; or share the track via a Twitter tweet.

To return to the previous screen, tap the Hide button at the top-right corner.

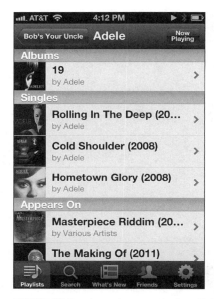

FIGURE 23.5   An artist page in Spotify Mobile.

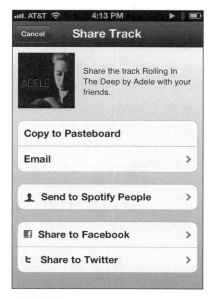

FIGURE 23.6   Sharing a track in Spotify Mobile.

Searching for Music

You can also search for tracks to stream from the Spotify service. You do this by tapping the Search tab at the bottom of the window.

The Search page consists of three tabs and a search box at the top. You conduct a search by entering a query into the search box with the iPhone's onscreen keyboard and then tapping the Search button.

As you can see in Figure 23.7, the results are now displayed on each of the three tabs. You see matching Tracks, Albums, and Artists. Tap a track to play it; tap an album to display the tracks in that album; or tap an artist name to display that artist's Spotify page.

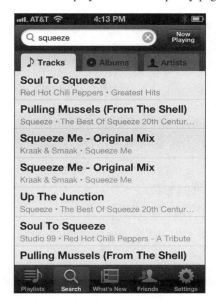

FIGURE 23.7   The results of a Spotify Mobile search.

Viewing What's New

Want to find out what's new in the world of music—and the world of Spotify? Tap the What's New tab to display the What's New page, shown in Figure 23.8. On this page you see Spotify's Top Tracks, New Releases, and News Feed (the latest news from Spotify). Tap an item to either play it or learn more.

FIGURE 23.8   Spotify Mobile's What's New page.

Sharing Friends' Music

When you tap the Friends tab, you see a list of all your Facebook friends who are also Spotify subscribers. When you tap the name of a friend, you see a list of the playlists this person has recently created, as shown in Figure 23.9. Tap an item to open the playlist; from there you can play the tracks in either standard or shuffle mode.

Listening in Offline Mode

As you learned in Lesson 15, "Playing Music Offline," you can listen to music when you're not connected to the Internet by entering Spotify's Offline mode. This is especially important with Spotify Mobile, as you often find yourself in situations (such as driving in your car or riding in a plane) where you don't have an active Internet connection.

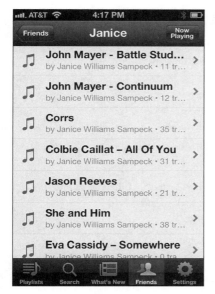

FIGURE 23.9   Viewing a friend's playlists.

Before you can listen to music offline, you have to activate a given playlist for Offline mode. To do this, open the playlist page on your iPhone and then turn the Available Offline switch to On.

Whenever your phone loses an Internet connection, Spotify Mobile automatically goes into Offline mode. You can then listen to those playlists you've previously activated for offline playback.

You can also activate Offline mode manually for your mobile device. This is great if your device is low on battery power and you want to conserve your charge.

To manually enter Offline mode on your mobile device, tap the Settings icon at the bottom of the Spotify screen. When the Settings screen appears, go to the Offline Mode section and turn the Offline Mode switch to On.

The Spotify Mobile app now enters Offline mode. Tap the Offline Mode switch to Off to return to normal listening mode.

Adjusting Settings

There are several other settings you might want or need to configure in the Spotify Mobile app. You access these settings by tapping the Settings tab.

Here's what you find on the Settings page, shown in Figure 23.10:

▶ **Offline Mode.** As previously described, this manually forces Spotify Mobile into Offline mode.

▶ **Private Session.** When enabled, this option deactivates all social sharing for the current session.

▶ **Scrobble to Last.fm.** Sends information about the tracks you play to the Last.fm service. (Learn more in Lesson 21, "Scrobbling Your Music to Last.fm.")

▶ **Show on Facebook.** Enabled by default; disable this setting to *not* send the tracks you play to your Facebook News Feed.

▶ **Hide Unplayable Tracks.** Enabled by default; disable this setting to view tracks you can't play on your mobile device.

▶ **Stream.** By default, Spotify Mobile uses a lower-quality stream to conserve wireless bandwidth; change to High Quality if you're on a fast Wi-Fi connection and want higher-quality playback.

▶ **Sync.** By default, Spotify uses a high-quality stream to sync music between your mobile device and PC. If you have a slow wireless connection, change this setting to Low Bandwidth.

▶ **Sync Over 2G/3G.** By default, Spotify only syncs tracks if you're on a Wi-Fi connection. If you also want to sync over your mobile network, enable this option.

▶ **Log Out.** Tap this to log out of Spotify on your mobile device.

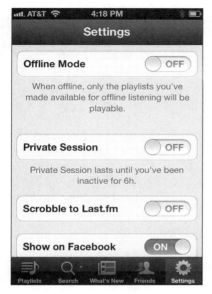

FIGURE 23.10   Configuring Spotify Mobile's settings.

Summary

In this lesson, you learned how to use Spotify on your iPhone. In the next
lesson you learn how to configure Spotify's preferences.

LESSON 24

Configuring Spotify

In this lesson, you learn how to configure Spotify's various options.

Editing Spotify Preferences

There are several configuration settings within Spotify that affect how the application works. These settings are all available on Spotify's Preferences page, shown in Figure 24.1. To access this page, pull down the Edit menu and select Preferences.

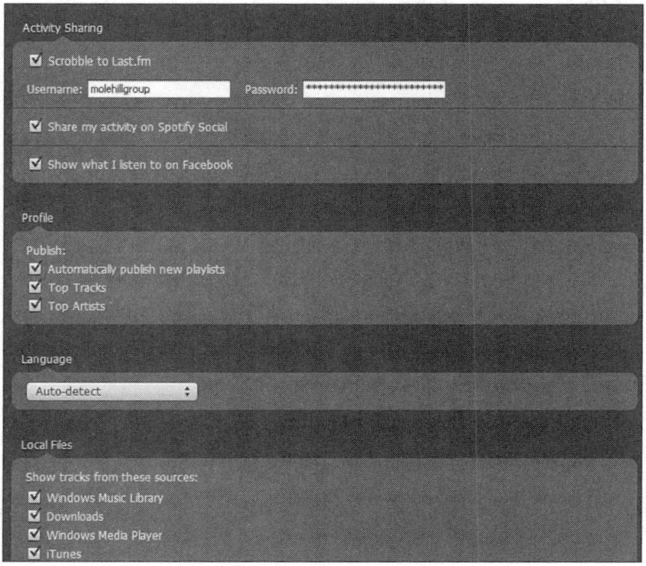

FIGURE 24.1 Spotify's Preferences page.

Controlling Preferences

Spotify's Preferences page is organized into several major sections. Let's examine each section individually.

Activity Sharing

The Activity Sharing section is where you configure how Spotify interacts with various social networks and applications. In particular, you can configure the following:

▶ **Scrobble to Last.fm.** Enable this option to transmit information about the music you play to the Last.fm service. (See Lesson 21, "Scrobbling Your Music to Last.fm," for more details.)

▶ **Share My Activity on Spotify Social.** Check this box to enable all of Spotify's social sharing features.

▶ **Show What I Listen to on Facebook.** Enable this option to transmit each track you play to your Facebook news feed.

Profile

The options in the Profile section determine what is displayed to other users in your public Spotify profile. You can opt to display or hide the following:

▶ **Automatically publish new playlists.** Displays any new playlists you create.

▶ **Top Tracks.** Displays your most listened-to songs.

▶ **Top Albums.** Displays your most listened-to albums.

Language

By default Spotify automatically detects which language your computer uses and uses that language in its display. You can, however, force Spotify to display in another language; pull down the list in the Language section and select from English, Spanish, French, German, or Dutch.

Local Files

The Local Files section is where you tell Spotify where to look for music files on your computer to import. Check those locations (folders) you want to import from; click the Add Source button to add other locations to the list.

Playback

The Playback section helps control the playback of your music. You can choose from the following options:

- ▶ **Set the Same Volume Level for All Tracks.** Helps equalize the volume level between overly loud and overly soft tracks.

- ▶ **Enable Hardware Acceleration.** You should disable this option if you have trouble with music playback, especially music "jumping" or fast forwarding of its own accord.

- ▶ **Hide Unplayable Tracks.** Check this option to not display those tracks you can't play on your computer—such as imported tracks on someone else's playlist.

- ▶ **High Quality Streaming.** By default, Spotify streams its tracks at 160kbps. If you subscribe to Spotify Premium or Unlimited, however, you can enable higher-quality streaming for some tracks at 320kbps. To take full advantage of this better-sounding music, however, you must have a reliably fast Wi-Fi/Internet connection. Disable this option if you have trouble playing back tracks on your Internet connection.

Cache

Spotify temporarily stores some of its streaming files on your computer's hard disk, to better play back those tracks. By default, Spotify uses no more than 10% of your computer's disk space for this cache. You can, however, specify the exact amount of disk space to be used by Spotify by adjusting the slider in the Cache section of the Preferences page. You can also change the location that Spotify uses for its cache.

Proxy

If you have trouble connecting to Spotify, you might need to manually enter new Proxy settings on the Preferences page. Consult your ISP, corporate IT staff, or Spotify's technical support for more details.

Social Network

If you want to unlink your Spotify and Facebook accounts, go to the Social Network section and click the Disconnect from Facebook button.

Open Spotify Automatically After You Log into the Computer

If you use Spotify a lot, you might want to launch Spotify automatically when you turn on your PC. You have three options in this final section of the Preferences page:

- **Open automatically.** Launches Spotify whenever you turn on your computer.

- **Open automatically, but minimized.** Launches Spotify when you turn on your computer, but minimizes the Spotify window.

- **Don't open automatically.** The default option, requires you to manually launch Spotify when you want to use the service.

Summary

In this lesson, you learned how to configure the options on Spotify's Preferences page. This also concludes this book—where you've learned how to get the most out of Spotify and discover a lot of terrific new music.

Index

G-H

I-K

N

Q-R